T0327918

PALETTE
mini

IRIDESCENT

Published and distributed by
viction:workshop ltd.

viction:ary™

viction:workshop ltd.
Unit C, 7/F, Seabright Plaza, 9–23 Shell Street,
North Point, Hong Kong SAR
Website: www.victionary.com
Email: we@victionary.com

 @victionworkshop
 @victionworkshop
Bē @victionary
 @victionary

Edited and produced by viction:ary

Creative direction by Victor Cheung
Book design by viction:workshop ltd.
Typeset in NB International Pro from Neubau

Second Edition
©2022, 2024 viction:workshop ltd.

ISBN 978-988-74628-3-5
Printed and bound in China

PREFACE

According to the Cambridge Dictionary, the word 'palette' may refer to the range of colours that an artist usually paints with on a canvas. Today, however, more than just the primary means of creative expression for wielders of the physical brush, its role has expanded to include that of an important digital tool for crafting meaningful solutions in design. On top of manifesting pure works of the imagination as it has always done, the palette has become a purveyor of infinite visual possibilities with the power to bridge art and commerce. Since the release of its first edition in 2012, viction:ary's PALETTE colour-themed series has become one of the most successful and sought-after graphic design reference collections for students and working professionals around the world; showcasing a thoughtful curation of compelling ideas and concepts revolving around the palette featured. In keeping with the needs and wants of the savvy modern reader, the all-new PALETTE mini Series has been reconfigured and rejuvenated with fresh content, for all intents and purposes, to serve as the intriguing, instrumental, and timeless source of inspiration that its predecessor was, in a more convenient size.

INTRO

There is something evocative about light that captivates viewers. While powerful all on its own, its magical properties are truly brought to life when it hits a holographic surface, propelling the imagination by shifting colours and form. Across time, many artists and designers have been inspired by iridescence to add an extra dimension to their creations. The Light and Space movement in the 1960s, which typically featured materials like glass and resin to play with light, volume, and scale, is often thought of as the beginnings of the holographic boom. Fast forward to today, even more possibilities exist for creative exploration, thanks to technology.

The timeless popularity of holographics in design likely stems from its ability to express a compelling story or concept even through minimal use, among others. Tsan Yu Yin's project 'Oyster Stout Trio' on PP. 228–233 is a shining example of this, where the iridescence of oyster shells informs UGLY HALF BEER's elegant bottle labels for its new range. Inspired by the centuries-old ritual of pairing oysters with stout and the relatively short history of their use in brewing, Tsan celebrates the products' unique ingredients—featuring rich coffee and chocolate flavours balanced by a touch of brine from a Chiayi oyster—with a simple but striking design that stands out on the shelves. Hong Kong-based studio THINGSIDID applied a similar line of thinking to their editorial work on PP. 010–013. For CoBo Social's book on 'Collected Writings By Artists On Artists', they decided on a holographic cover to aptly encompass the colourful tales and personalities highlighted by the contents. Studio South, a design consultancy based in Auckland, also chose iridescence as the perfect metaphor in redeveloping their visual identity (PP. 032–035). The team set out to create 'a clean brand that reflected the progression of their approach', where every project is carefully considered, and collateral execution is key. Paired with a bold sans-serif typeface and monochromatic colours, the outcome speaks volumes about their evolution by demonstrating a clever balance of subtlety and statement-making design. In Patricia Urquiola's Shimmer range for Glas Italia (PP. 590–597), iridescence was used to characterise an ethereal quality in the furniture. Depending on the vantage point of the viewer and the angle of the light, each piece is seen to display an infinite variety of nuances due to its multi-coloured finish. The added quality of lightness also elevated the range of round tables made.

In art, the flexibility of holographic effects has enabled creatives to push aesthetic boundaries and allow viewers to derive different meanings from the work produced. In conjunction with Serpentine Galleries' celebration of the world-renowned Pavilion commission's 15th anniversary in 2015 (PP. 612–618), it showcased an 'amorphous, double-skinned polygonal structure' designed by award-winning studio selgascano. Featuring several different entry/exit points through a 'secret corridor' between the outer and inner layers of the structure into the Pavilion's stained-glasslike interior, the architects set out to connect their architectural interests with nature, allowing the public to experience the Pavilion through elements like lightness, form, transparency, sensitivity, and change. Similarly, François Ollivier's 'bittersweet' experimental set of installations that were created during the pandemic lockdowns in 2020 (PP. 564–573) featured a rainbow-reflective fabric to represent the absurd, dream-like quality of recent events. In 'reinventing' rooms that people typically spent the most time in like the bedroom and bathroom, 'Times of Reflection' provoked viewers into seeing everyday spaces through a perspective-bending lens.

Ultimately, no matter where the trends lead, iridescence is here to stay as a tool for boundless creativity and luminous sparks of inspiration.

JENNIFER YOUNG
STUDIO

YOUNG

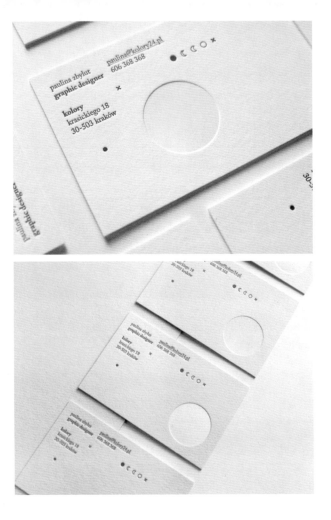

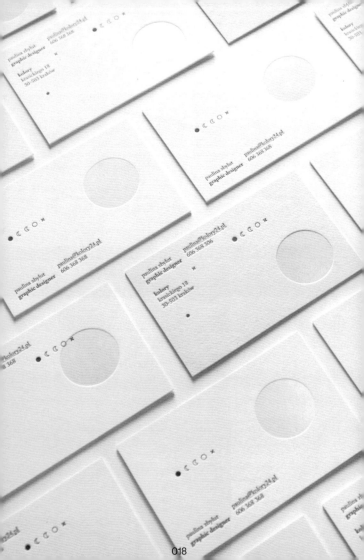

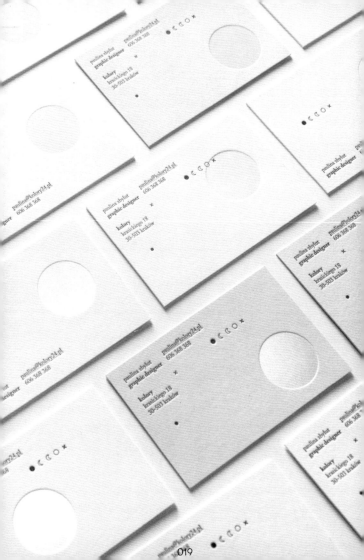

019

020

021

제도론: 변화무쌍한 생명체
데릭 매트레이버스

THE INSTITUTIONAL THEORY:
A PROTEAN CREATURE
DEREK MATRAVERS

저자의 소개
데릭 매트레이버스 영국 개방 대학교(Open
University) 철학과 교수이다. 게임브리지 대학교
다른 칼리지에서 연구원으로 재직하기도 했다.
미학, 윤리학, 심리 철학 등을 연구 영역으로
삼으며『예술과 감정(Art and Emotions』등 7가지
사례 연구를 통한 예술 철학의 소 Reconstituting
Philosophy of Art in Eight Case Studies,
『허구와 서사(Fiction and Narrative』
『공감(Empathy』등의 저서가 있다.

옮긴이 소개
김천돌 고려대학교에서 경제학과 철학을,
영 대학원에서 시경 철학을 전공했다. 현재 본
대학교 철학과에서 박사 과정에 예비 중이다.
옮긴 책으로는『초기 그리스 철학(上하)』
등이 있으며『예술의 변증법(공역)을 포함한
스캔돌드 철학백과의 함께 및 서양 철학의
논문도 몇 개 번역했다.

제도론: 변화무쌍한 생명체
데릭 매트레이버스

THE INSTITUTIONAL THEORY:
A PROTEAN CREATURE
DEREK MATRAVERS

...urned two and we'd like to
... thanks for being part of our
... To help us celebrate we invite
... join us at the Hesketh Tavern
...ere you can help yourself to some
...ood and a few drinks. We'd love to
see you there.

Thursday 1st Sept, 4-7pm
Hesketh Tavern, 93 Holme Road,
Clewedbs Holme, OK8 6JC
RSVP dawn@dawncreative.co.uk

Dawn Creative

Maximage Color Combinations
Edition of 500 copies, 2017
ECAL/University of Art and Design Lausanne

This book is a tool for designers, artists and printers who are interested in personalized and unique color palettes. Created using between 2 and 5 spot colors, over 120 combinations were generated directly in the offset press by interfering with the ink unit. This unorthodox color-mixing technique helped to create more than 450 spot colors evolving over the 500 different books, turning each one into a set of totally unique combinations.

The book explores how different colors and hues can interact together, and how they can merge from one to another. Without any chapters or formulas, colors travel from shiny to matte, blue to celadon, frozen to boiling, reflective to absorbent, dark light to brain grey, spectral to metameric, sunshine to neon, from Atlanta to Albertville, or from Leipzig to Juba via Napoli and back again, in an attempt to tell infinite stories.

The user will not find here this year's hot color nor the trends for next season. Rather, each page tells a different story that each user can relate to, reinterpret or reappropriate in their own way.

This publication follows "Maximage Formula Guide" and "Maximage Raster Guide", and is part of the "Workflow" Research Project (R&D). It was conceived and printed during a workshop at ECAL held by Maximage and the printer Thomi Wolfensberger, Zurich.

With the participation of Giacomo Bastianelli, Mélanie Blanc, Victoire Bornhauser, Pauline Brocart, Benoît Brun, Juliette Caillault, Sebastian Davila, Ariane Delahaye, Sarah Di Venosa, Jenny Donnet-Descartes, Loïc Dupasquier, Laurence Favez, Boris Fernandez, Loana Gatti, Clément Gicquel, Marine Giraudo, Amaury Hamon, Pamela Jaton, Valentin Kaiser, Sereina Kessler, Thomas Le Provost, Vidal Mateos, Dimitri Nägele, Sophie Soullé, Laetitia Troilo, Laura-Issé Tusevo, Gwendolyn Ummel, Sabrina Vega and Matthieu Visentin.

"Workflow" is a research project led at ECAL by David Keshavjee, Guy Meldem, Tatiana Rihs, Julien Tavelli and supported by the HES-SO/University of Applied Sciences Western Switzerland.

Printed at ECAL in 2017 by Benjamin Plantier, Thomi Wolfensberger and Maximage.

www.ecal.ch
www.colorlibrary.ch

Hes·so

ISBN: 978-2-9701157-9-3

Artists
on
Artists

CoBo
Social
→
Collected
Writings
By
Artists
On
Artists

et al.

CO
BO

CoBo
Social
→
Collected
Writings
By
Artists
On
Artists

et al.

Artists
on
Art

037

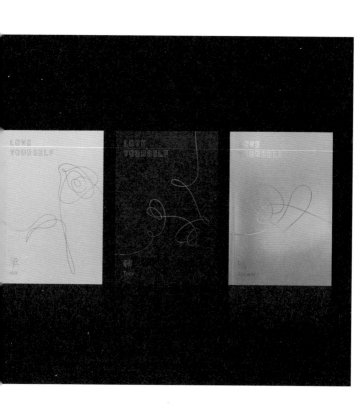

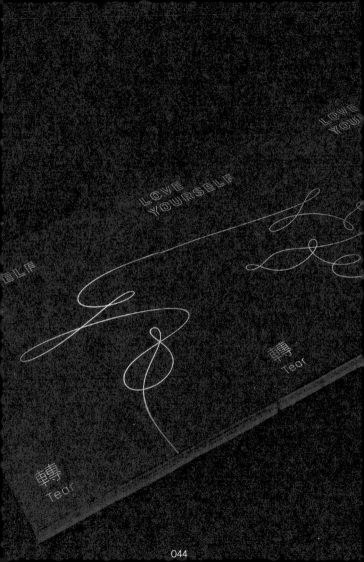

轉
Tear

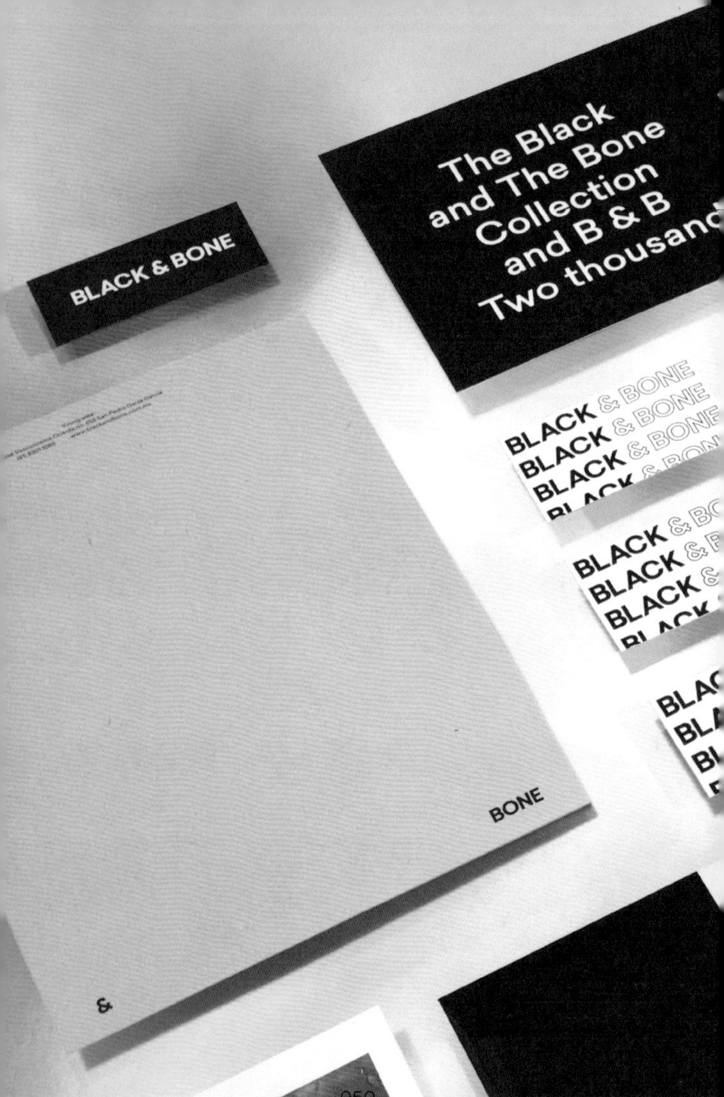

BLACK & BONE

The Black
and The Bone
Collection
and B & B
Two thousand

BLACK & BONE
BLACK & BONE
BLACK & BONE

BLACK & B
BLACK &
BLACK

BLA
BL
B

BONE

&

BLACK & BONE

Two thousand
and Seventeen
The Black Bone
and The Black
Collection B & B
seventeen
Young wear
Two thousand

Black and Bone · Young wear · Two thousand seventeen
Opening night — Young wear · B & B
Presenting the Black Collection, The Bone Collection and B & B
H. B. R. · April 8, 2017
D. D. D. · P. D. D. · Q.
Sonsontorn 82 · H. · Mexico

789589947295252534281

BLACK & BONE

BLACK & BONE

ONE
ONE
BONE
BONE

BONE

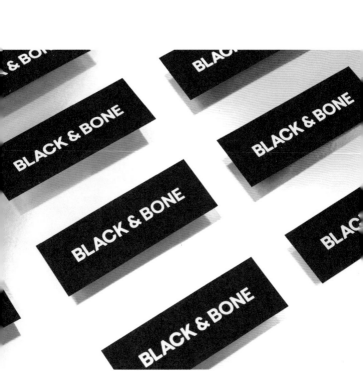

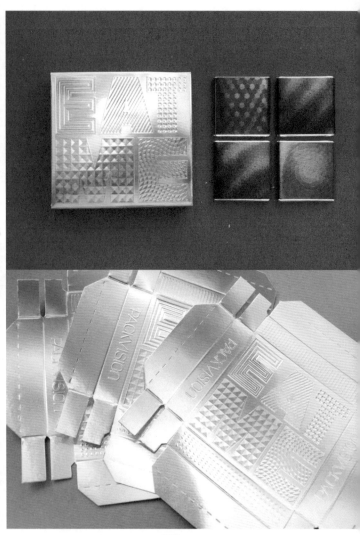

054

EINLADUNG
ERÖFFNUNG

HASLERWEIN
PANORAMA

Wir feiern die Eröffnung des HaslerWein Panoramas. Am **Mittwoch 29. Juni 2016** weihen wir unser neues Terrassen-Lokal offiziell ein. Dazu laden wir Dich und eine Begleitperson Deiner Wahl herzlich ein.

Um Anmeldung unter hasler@haslerwein.ch bis am 17. Juni 2016 wird gebeten.

Der Anlass findet in der Weinkellerei Hasler am Bielweg 32 in Tüscherz-Alfermée statt. Da nur wenige Parkplätze vorhanden sind, steht ab Bahnhof Tüscherz zwischen 17.00 und 17.30 Uhr ein Shuttle-Service zum Weingut hinauf zur Verfügung. Für die Rückkehr zum Bahnhof ist der Shuttle ebenso verfügbar.

Wir freuen uns auf Deinen Besuch.
Mit besten Grüssen

Lukas Hasler & Team

Programm:
ab 17.00 Uhr   Apéro
17.45 Uhr   Musikalische Begrüssung und Vorstellen des Konzepts
18.00 Uhr   Begrüssung mit regionalen Spezialitäten
18.15 Uhr   Verkostigung mit regionalen A&J
18.45 Uhr   Musikalisches Intermezzo A&J
19.00 Uhr   Gemütliches Beisammensein

MITTWOCH
29. JUNI 2016

WEINKELLEREI
HASLER

058

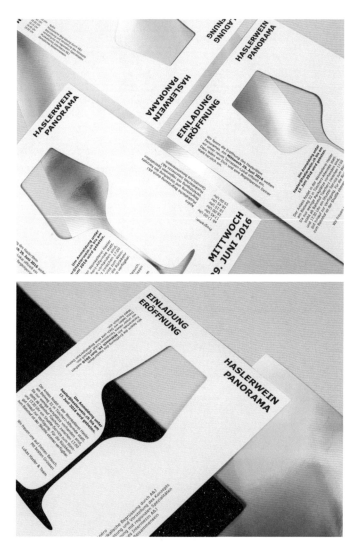

059

HASLERWEIN
PANORAMA

EINLADUNG
ERÖFFNUNG

Wir feiern die Eröffnung des HaslerWein
Panoramas. Am **Mittwoch 29. Juni 2016** weihen
wir unser neues Terrassen-Lokal offiziell ein.
Dazu laden wir Dich und eine Begleitperson Deiner
Wahl herzlich ein.

MITTWOCH
29. JUNI 2016

Programm:

ab 17.00 Uhr
17.45 Uhr
18.00 Uhr
18.15 Uhr
19.00 Uhr

Apéro
Musikalische Begrüssung durch A8J
Begrüssung und Vorstellung des Konzepts
Verkostigung mit regionalen Spezialitäten
Musikalisches Intermezzo A8J
Gemütliches Beisammensein

...u 17.30 ... Kellerei Hasler
... Bahnhof ...rkplätze ...erz-Alfermée vorhanden sind, statt,
gut hinauf zur Verfügung. Für die Rückkehr
zum Bahnhof ist der Shuttle-Service zwischen 17.00 Shuttle ebenso verfügbar.

Wir freuen uns auf Deinen Besuch.
Mit besten Grüssen

Lukas Hasler & Team

WEINKELLEREI
HASLER

061

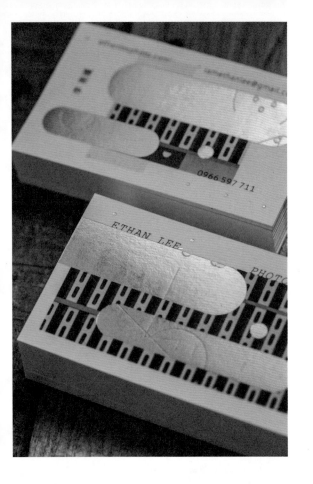

ETHAN LEE PHOTOGRAPHY

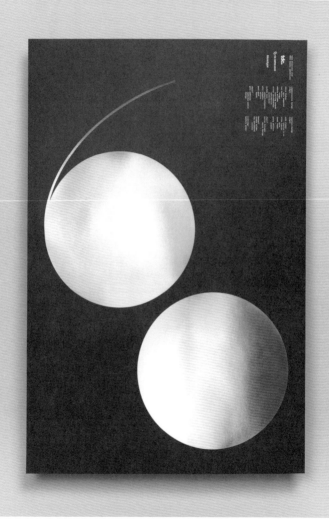

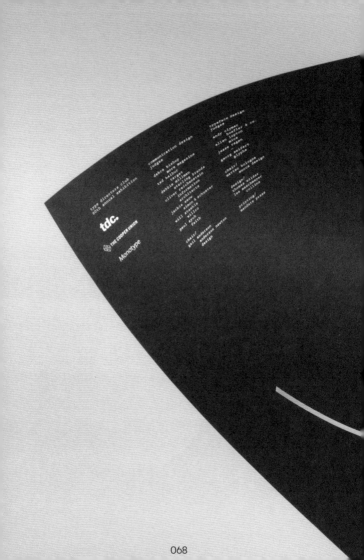

type directors club
60th annual exhibition

tdc.

THE COOPER UNION

Monotype

communication design
judges

debra bishop
gary mazzanico
target
debbie millman
sterling brands
oliver reichenstein
information
architects
jackie simon schuster
will staehle
unusual co
paul sitio
gpo
faith

chair/
gail anderson
design

typeface design
judges

andy clymer
hoefler & co.
allen hoptor
jesse ragan
xyz type
georg seifert
glyphs

chair/
matteo bologna
mucca design

design/
thomas wilder
lev maschinov
collins

printing/
sandwig press

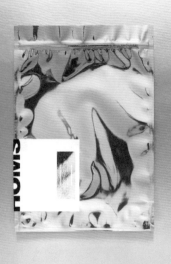

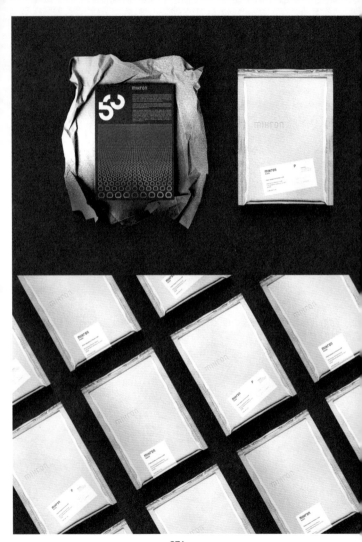

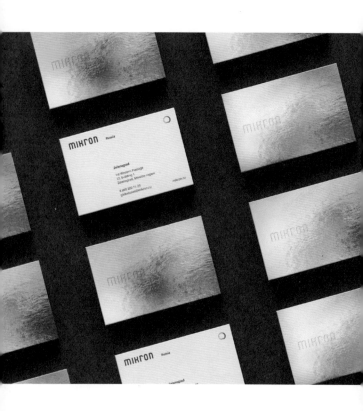

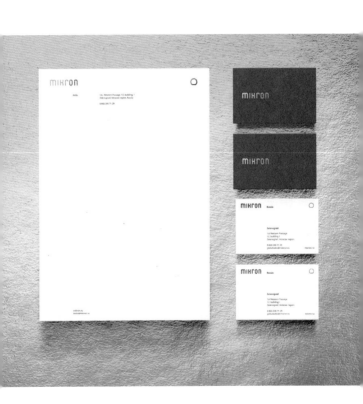

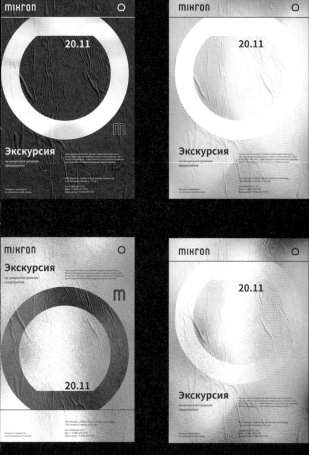

SHINE ON
YOU CRAZY
DIAMOND

SPHYNX

BE A
BORN
UNICORN
IN A FIELD
OF HORSES

SPHYNX

DON'T
LET
ANYONE
DULL YOUR
SPARKLE

SPHYNX

PINK IS MY
SIGNATURE
COLOR

SPHYNX

3 IN 1 TRAVEL RAZOR

PINK IS MY
SIGNATURE
COLOR

S P H Y N X

DON'T LET
ANYONE
DULL YOUR
SPARKLE

S P H Y N X

086

SHINE ON
YOU CRAZY
DIAMOND

SPHYNX

LEAVE
A SPARKLE
WHEREVER
YOU GO

SPHYNX

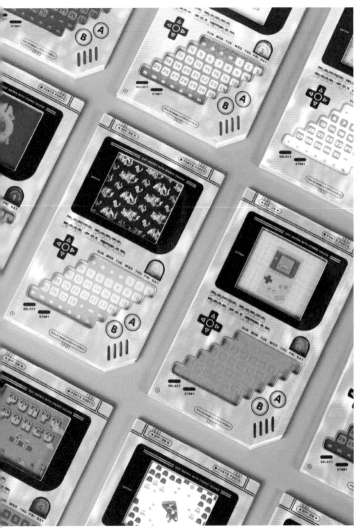

089

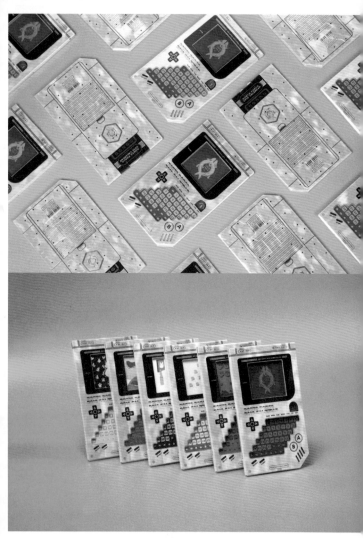

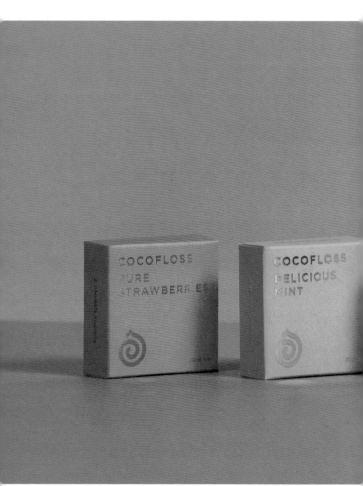

COCOFLOSS
FRESH
COCONUT

32 yd floss

COCOFLOSS
CARA CARA
ORANGE

2 month supply

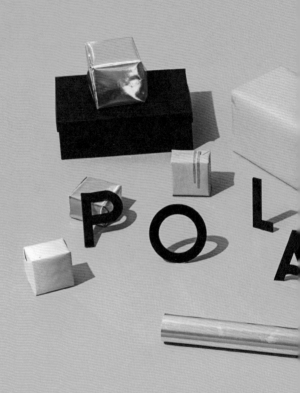

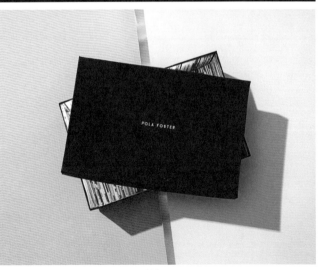

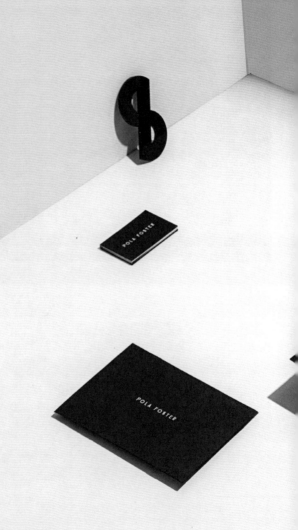

POLA FOSTER

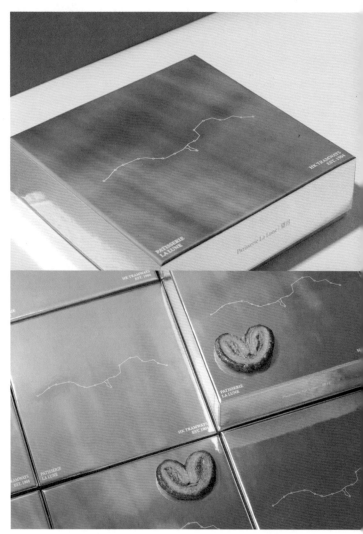

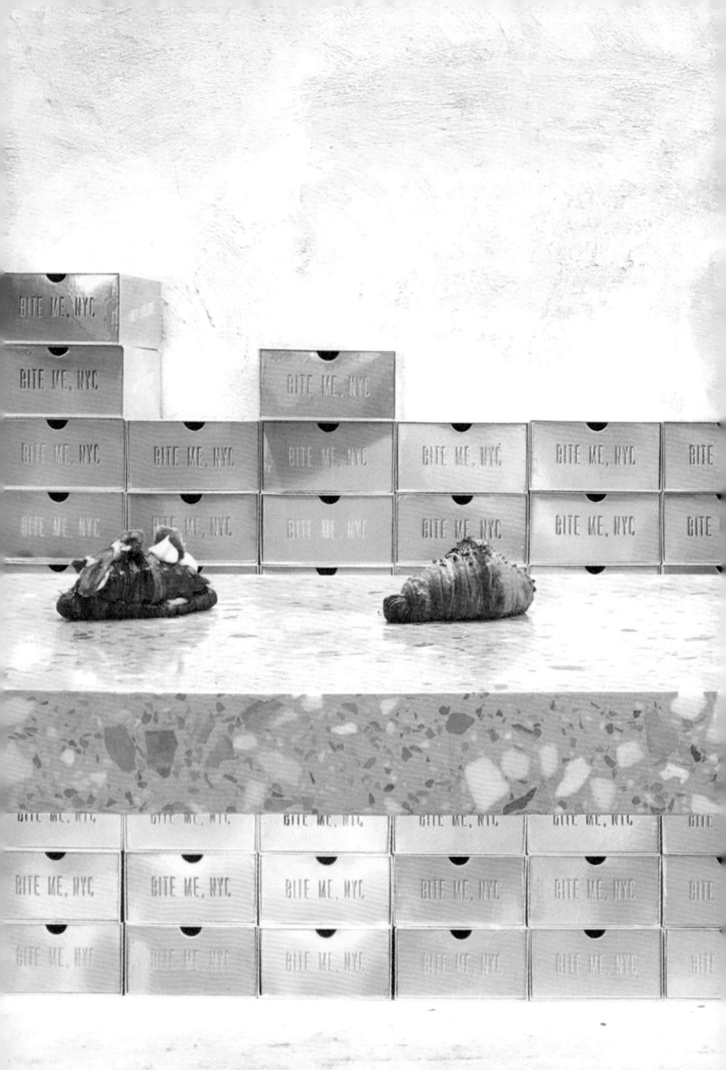
BITE ME, NYC

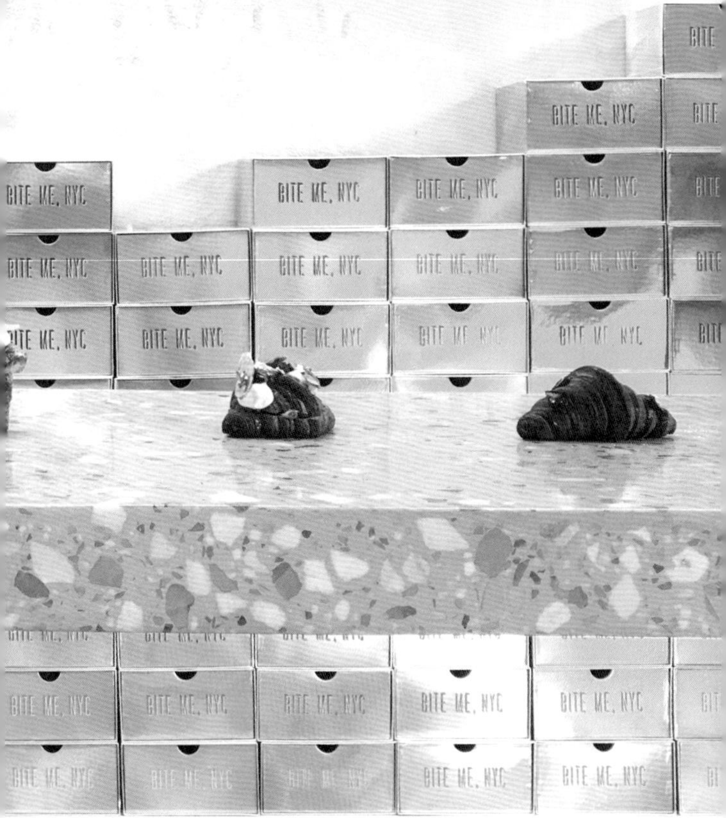
BITE ME, NYC

SUPERMOON

Daniel Barkle[1]

Graphic Designer

07398 252 612
hello(at)barkle.co

barkle.co
(at)danbarkle

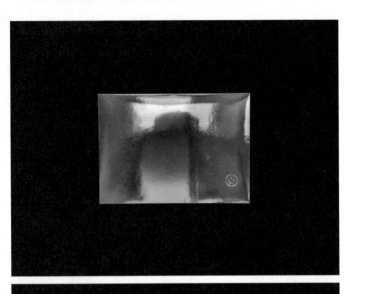

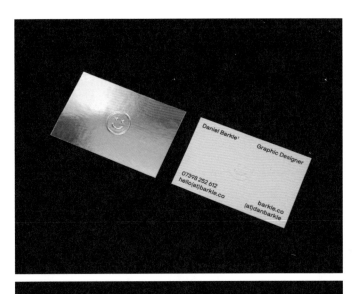

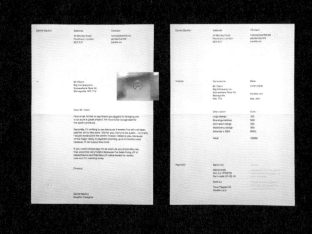

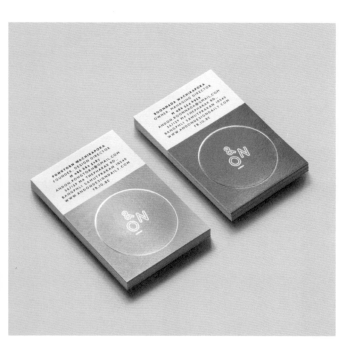

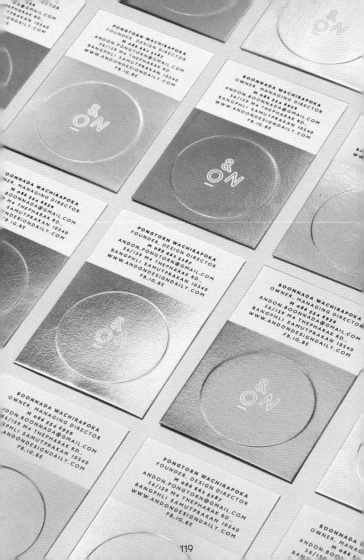

121

DESIGN
GRAPHIQUE
DIGITAL

DIRECTION
CRÉATIVE
ARTISTIQUE

2015

Design + Art Direction

Irradié

"Iridescence is part of our studio's visual identity. We wanted to play with the reflections of light and shadows on our business cards."

Irradié

STUDIO
DE
CRÉATION

DESIGN
GRAPHIQUE
& DIGITAL

DIRECTION
CRÉATIVE
ARTISTIQUE

2015

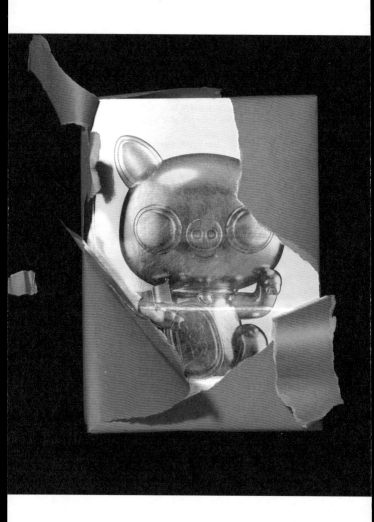

british
high school
of art &
design

Британские
программы

british high school of art & design.

2010.

british
high school
of art & de
britishdesign

british art & design

think   cre   apply

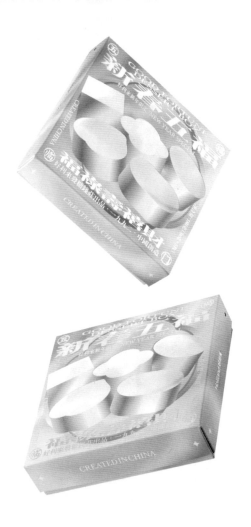

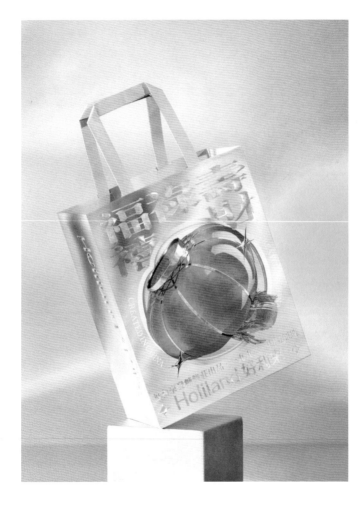

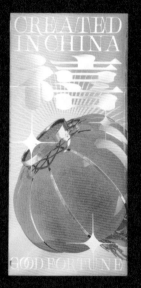

Good things
are coming

ROUXROU
XROUXROU

Good things
are coming

ROUX ROUX
ROUX ROUX

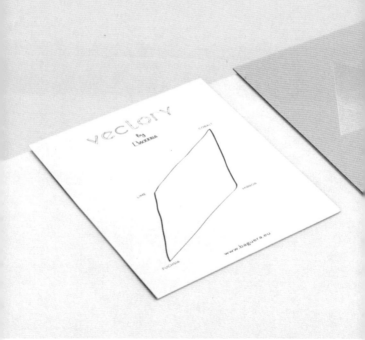

169

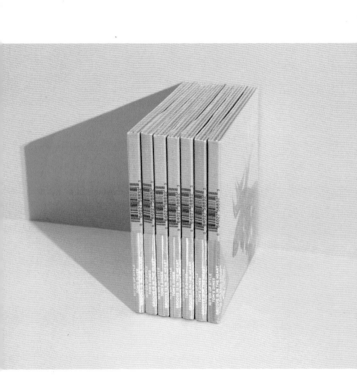

THE
LOST

WONDERS OF
THE WORLD

FINGERS

ALBUM DISPONIBLE dès MAINTENANT.
LANCEMENT-SPECTACLE le 8 MAI au BELMONT
PRÉSENTÉ PAR MONTREAL SPEAKEASE ELECTROSWING.
THELOSTFINGERS.COM

WONDERS OF
THE WORLD

THE
LOST

ALBUM DISPONIBLE dès MAINTENANT.
LANCEMENT-SPECTACLE le 8 MAI au BELMONT
PRÉSENTÉ PAR MONTREAL SPEAKEASE ELECTROSWING.
THELOSTFINGERS.COM

FINGERS

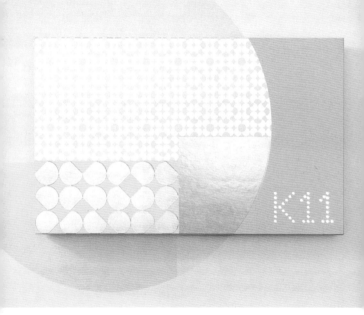

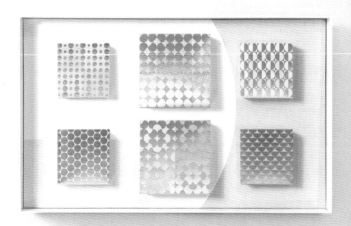

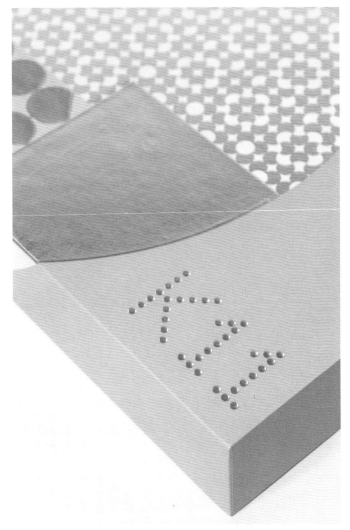

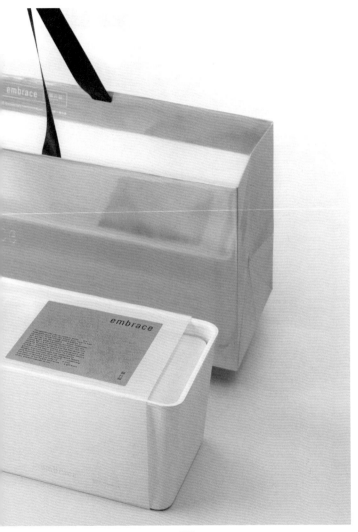

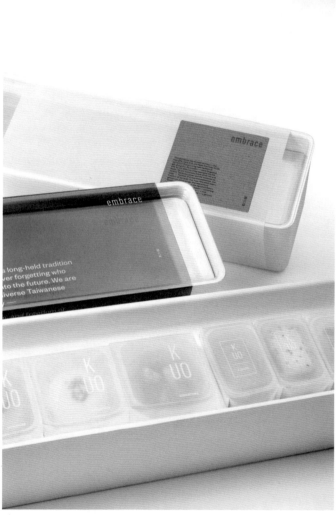

embrace

embrace

a long-held tradition
ver forgetting who
to the future. We are
iverse Taiwanese

Kuo Yuan Ye has carried on Taiwa
of gift-giving into the present — n
we are while marching resolutely i
immensely proud of our rich and c
values and the freedoms we enjoy

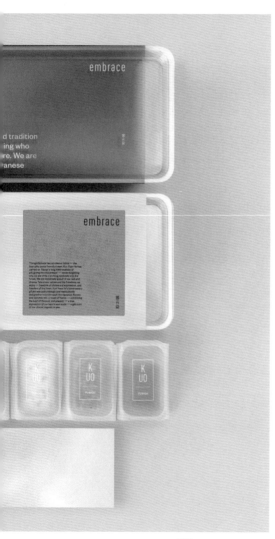

embrace

d tradition
ing who
re. We are
anese

embrace

Though times has ushered in brave — the
best gifts come from the heart. Kuo Yuan Ye has
carried on Taiwan's long-held tradition of
gift-giving into the present — never forgetting
who we are while enriching ourselves into the
future. We are constantly proud of our rich and
diverse Taiwanese culture and the freedom we
enjoy — freedom of choice and expression, and
freedom of the heart. Kuo Yuan Ye's boxes every
giftset was painstakingly and meticulously
designed to nourish open the signature flavors
and varieties with a touch of Taiwan — combining
the best of the past and present — a true
expression of our hearts and souls — a gift sent
in the utmost regards to you.

K
UO

K
UO

Borealica

-Bº

L - V   S
10 AM - 7 PM   9 AM - 2 PM

Av. Colorado 240 Oriente Loc.23
Colonia del Valle, San Pedro Garza García
NL - MX CP 66220

-Bº

Borealica es el nombre comercial del
primer studio de crioterapia de cuerpo
entero en la Ciudad de Monterrey

-8
cryotherapy, beauty & he
+52 (81) 1968 22
www.borealica.com

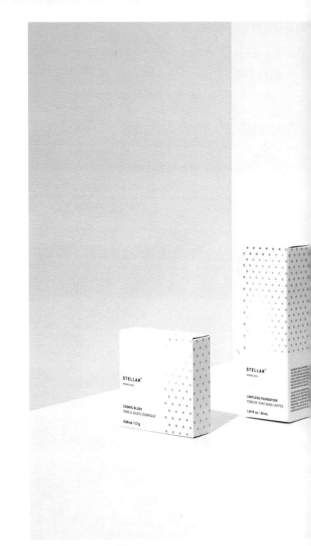

STELLAR*
MODÈLE CIEL

COSMIC BLUSH
FARD À JOUES COSMIQUE

0.06 oz / 1.7 g

STELLAR*
MODÈLE CIEL

LIMITLESS FOUNDATION
FOND DE TEINT SANS LIMITES

1.01 fl. oz / 30 mL

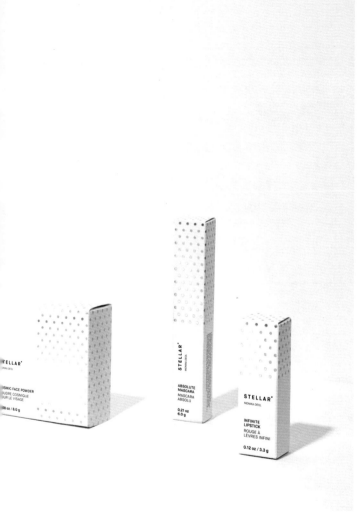

STELLAR*
MONIKA DEOL

SMIC FACE POWDER
UDRE COSMIQUE
UR LE VISAGE

28 oz / 8.0 g

STELLAR*
MONIKA DEOL

ABSOLUTE
MASCARA
MASCARA
ABSOLU

0.21 oz
6.0 g

STELLAR*
MONIKA DEOL

INFINITE
LIPSTICK
ROUGE À
LÈVRES INFINI

0.12 oz / 3.3 g

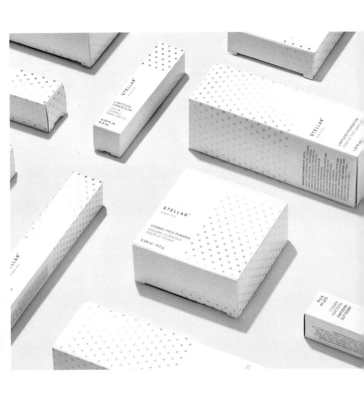

196

199

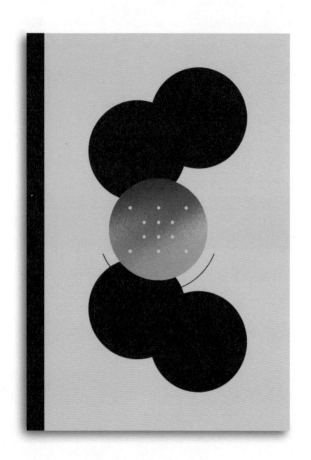

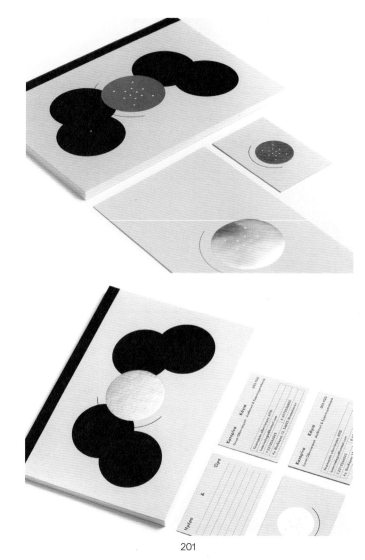

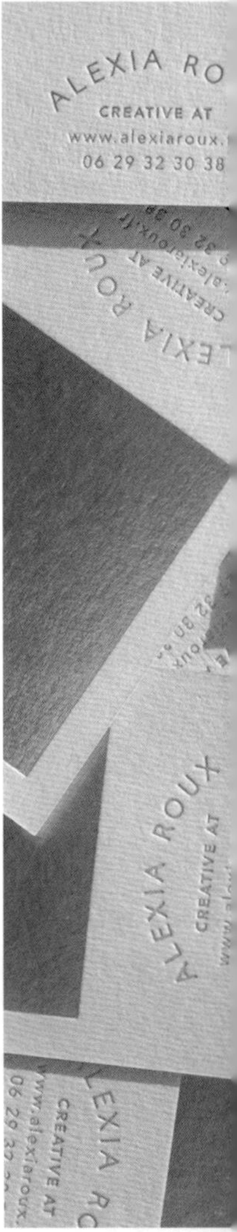
CREATIVE AT
06 29 32 30 38

"Iridescence is a process that elicits a physical and emotional response from the viewer. It encourages users to interact with it, to touch it, to move it. It feels alive."

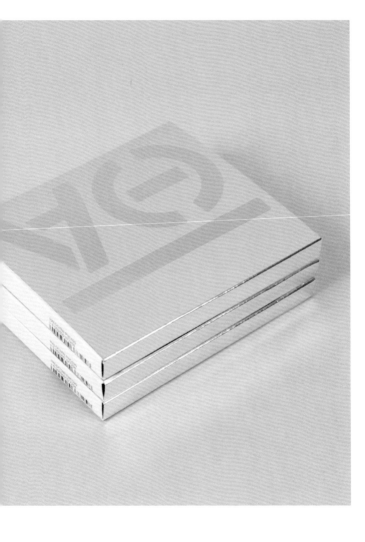

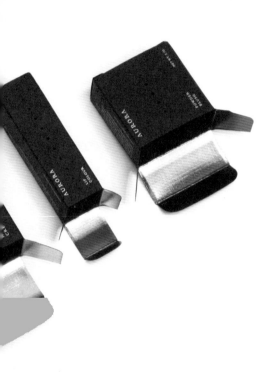

PROJECT—
CHARISMA

NAOMI IS A JAPANESE FEMININE NAME THAT MEANS WISE
AND BEAUTIFUL. SHE REPRESENTS THE CHARMING WOMAN OF
INTELLIGENCE, WISDOM AND SOPHISTICATION.

satomi

satomi

HAND
CREAM
50ml e 1.69fl oz

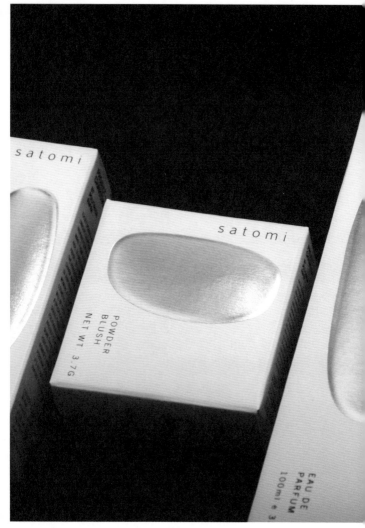

satomi

satomi

POWDER
BLUSH
NET WT 3.7G

EAU DE
PARFUM
100ml e 3

satomi

HAND
CREAM
50ml e 1.69s o...

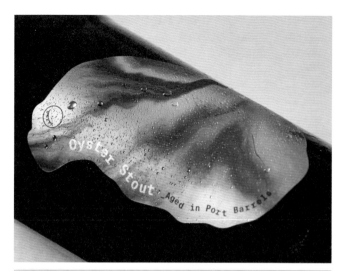

Oyster Stout · Aged in a blend of Bourbon and Rye Barrels

LUX
NATURALIS
GALA

6:00PM COCKTAILS & GALLERY TOURS
7:15PM DINNER & REMARKS
8:30PM DESSERT & DANCING

30 SEPT '16
6PM – 10PM

OF ART

LIVE ARTISTIC
ENTERTAINMENT
WITH MUSIC BY
THE DAVE STEPHENS BAND

MUSEUM

CREATIVE BLACK TIE
COMPLIMENTARY VALET

SPENCER

SPENCER MUSEUM OF ART
UNIVERSITY OF KANSAS
1301 MISSISSIPPI STREET
LAWRENCE, KS 66045

LUX
NAT
C

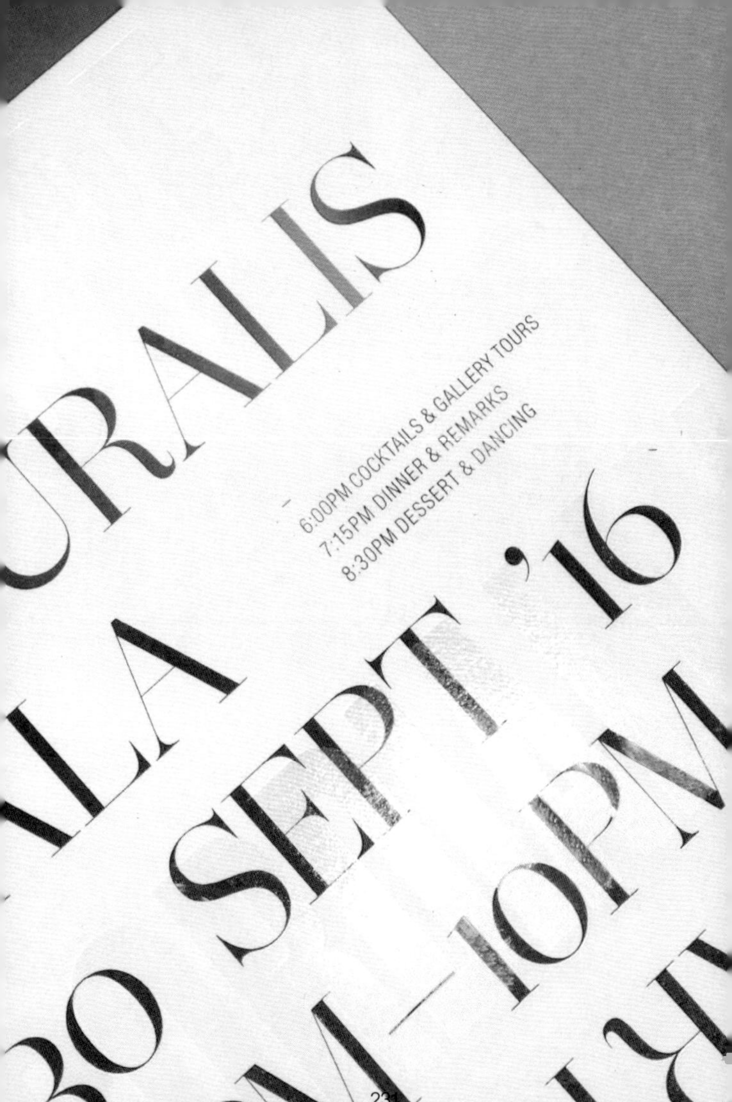

CRALIS

URALIS

ALA

30

SEPT '16

PM—10PM

6:00PM COCKTAILS & GALLERY TOURS
7:15PM DINNER & REMARKS
8:30PM DESSERT & DANCING

Derek Jarman

CHROMA

KSIĘGA

KOLORÓW

Derek Jarman

CHROMA

KSIĘGA

KOLORÓW

KURZ
COLLECTION
©2020/21

KURZ

KURZ

KURZ
CO

KURZ

KURZ
COLLECTION
©2020/21

WHAT IS FOIL?

01

03

"Iridescence is about manipulating or contemplating by searching for the right angle to catch the right light."

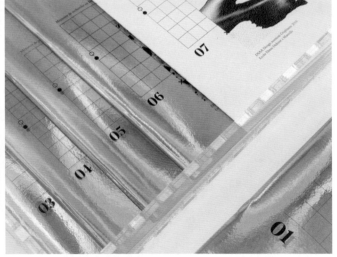

244

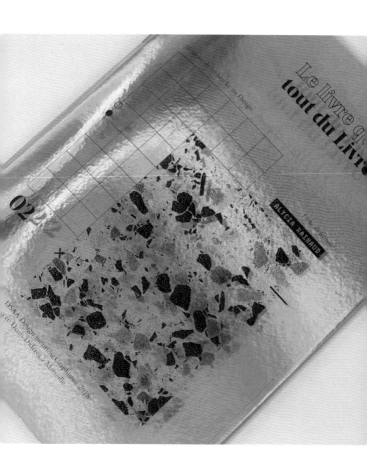

Maison de recherche en Design

Le livre q[...]
tout du Livr[...]

Fiche de lecture

ALYCIA RAINAUD

02

DSAA Design mention Graphisme
[...]rée Denis Diderot, Marseille 2018

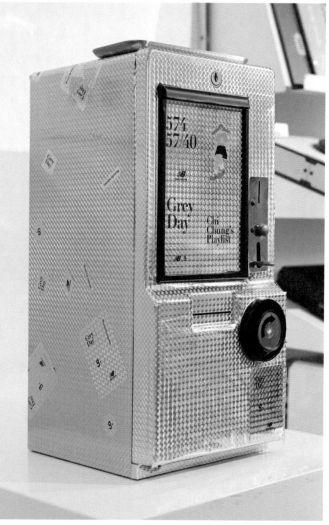

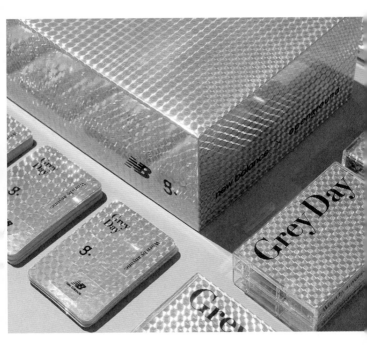

250

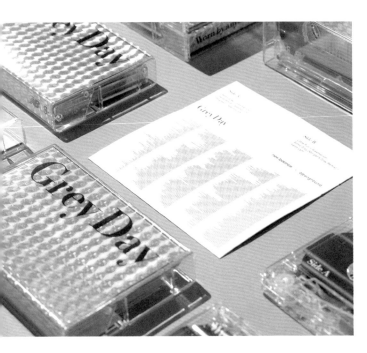

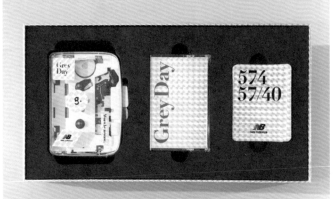

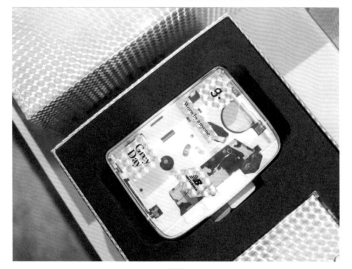

253

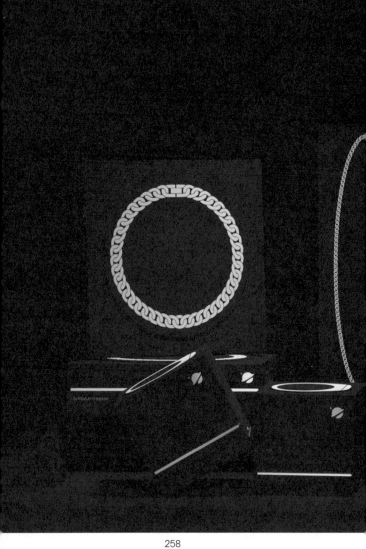

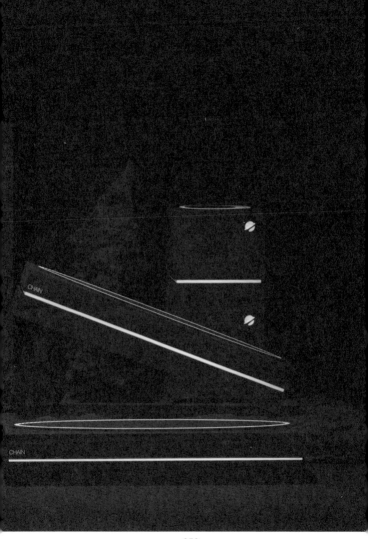

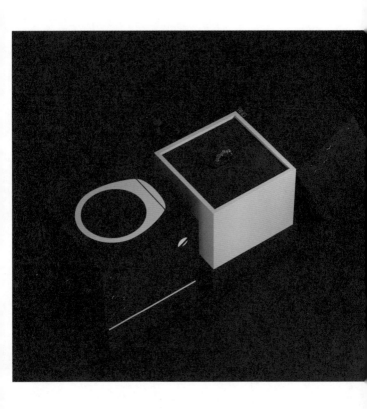

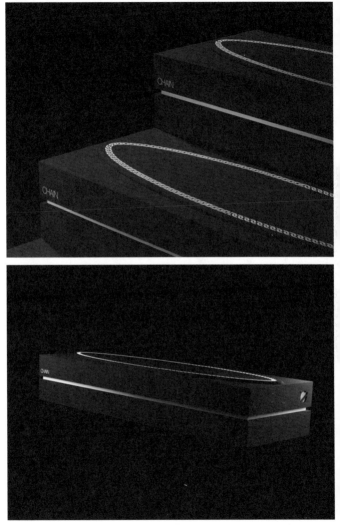

263

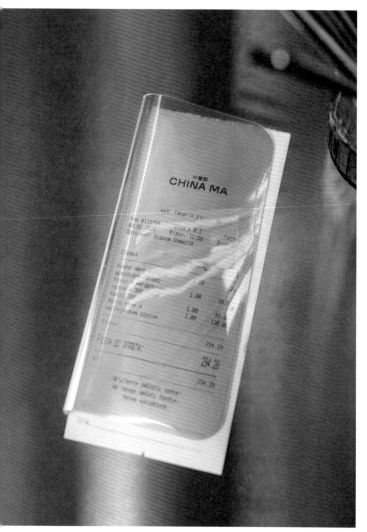

中餐館
CHINA MA

вул. Георгія Кірпи...

Чек #118764   Стіл # 9.1
01.02.2020   Відкр. 12:50   Гості:
Офіціант: Будков Олексій   Доч...

Страва

Комплімент Господ...   Кільть
шоколадне ...иво   ...00
Какао з мигдальни...   ...2...
...олоко 300   1.00   98.0...
Какао 300
...ма кекс з   1.00   56.0...
пасхурваим соусом   1.00   138.0...

Разом...   294.20

РАЗОМ ДО ОПЛАТИ: 294.20

                        294.20

                        294.20

Запрошуємо любити чужих і
не тільки любіти, Бровін...
чума китайська

273

YOU WERE BORN FOR THIS

ASTROLOGY FOR RADICAL
SELF-ACCEPTANCE

"Chani" YOU WERE BORN FOR THIS

CHANI NICHOLAS

279

balmerhaelen.ch

Rendez-
vous
des
créa
teurs   25 +
       26
       octo
       bre
       2017

nest

Chaus
sée
de la
Guin
guette
10

rdvcreateurs.ch

1800 Vevey

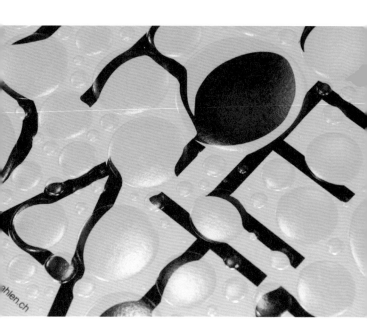

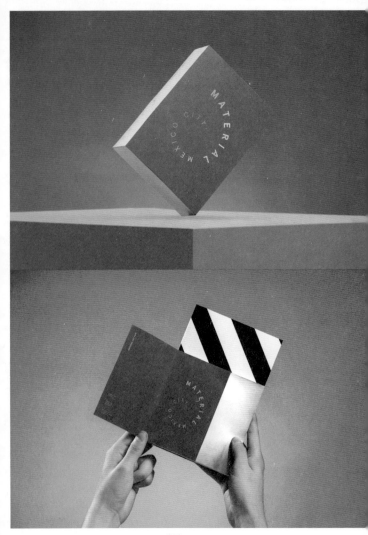

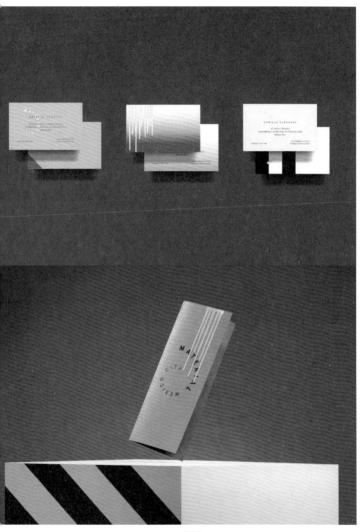

283

GERMAN / ENGLISH

um

HIC DESIGN \ 03.18

14,30 €
16,50

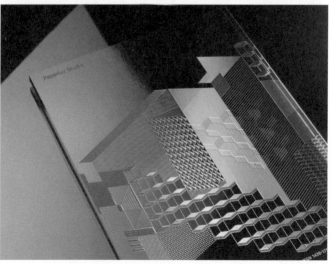

Greetings from
Poland!

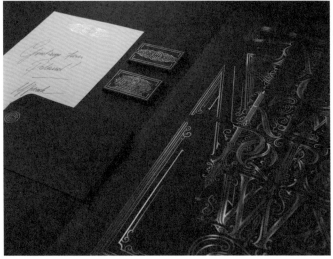

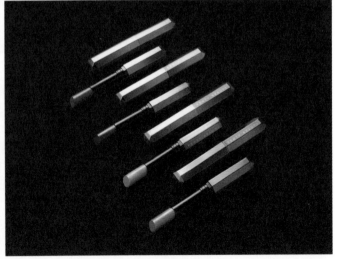

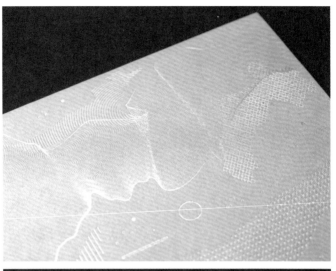

Much feeling
little thinking

Ivana Wong
王菀之

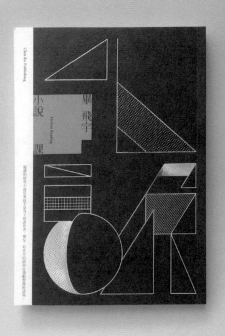

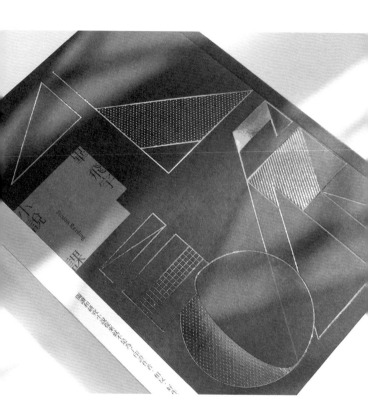

Fiction Reading

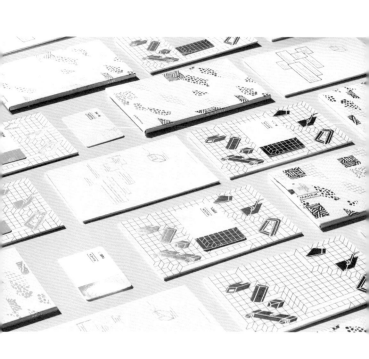

310

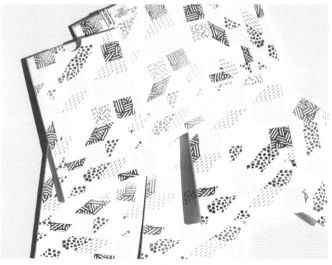

"It is easy to induce an interaction by using iridescence even when designing on stationary materials."

4. 매벌레
라이프

1ST. ALBUM
EDITION NO. /5●●

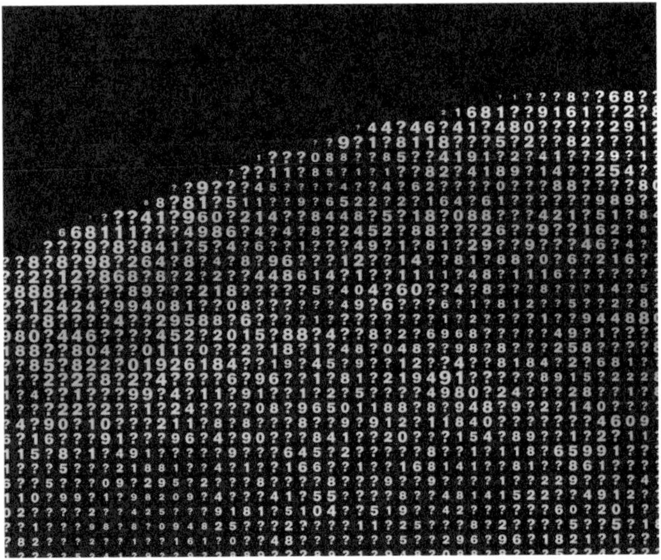

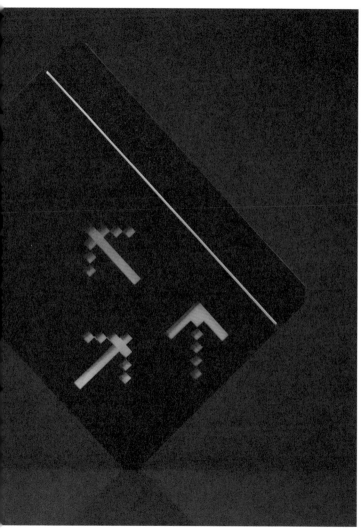

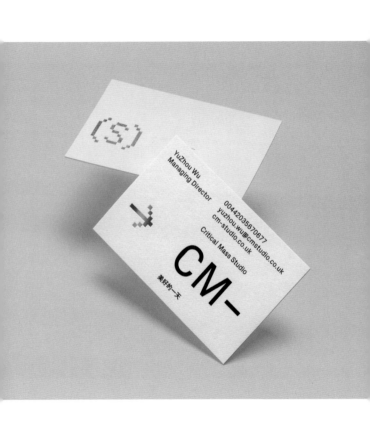

(5)

Yuzhou Wu
Managing Director

00442035670677
yuzhou.wu@cmstudio.co.uk
cm-studio.co.uk

Critical Mass Studio

CM—

美好的一天

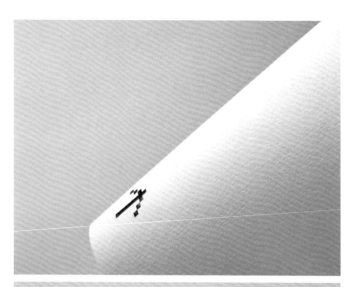

"Iridescence particularly acts as a powerful tool to metaphorically represent diversity. When placed in different environments, it transforms and mixes colour so uniquely and unexpectedly."

Holography.

Holography.

olography.

Holography.

S

G

January 2016
Tate Modern, L...
Discover mor...
otherodern...

A retrospective celebration
of underground music,
explored through
type & motion.

TATE

331

there's seen a return to what the real essence of   was, generating a young fan base, returning back to the original sound, the roots".

Jamie
Adenuga

"Eskimo was the dance, Boy In Da Corner, Home Sweet Home. They were the mark. We didn't care about anything else."

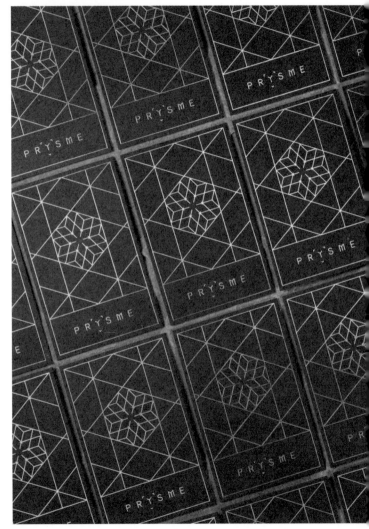

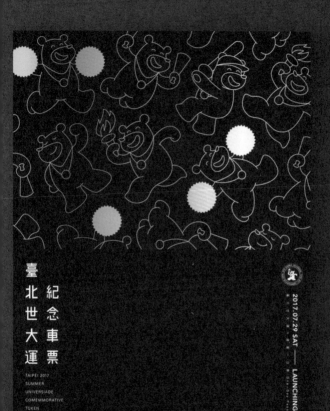

臺北世大運 紀念車票

TAIPEI 2017
SUMMER
UNIVERSIADE
COMEMMORATIVE
TOKEN

2017.07.29 SAT —— LAUNCHING

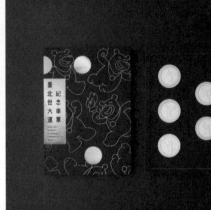

341

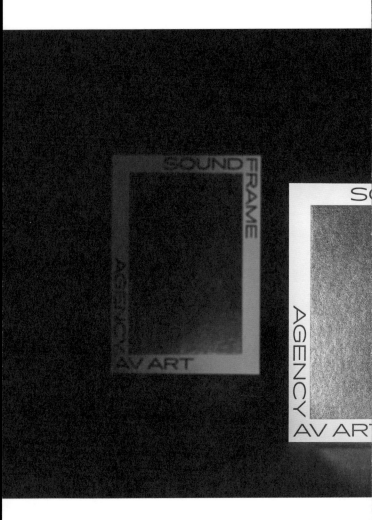

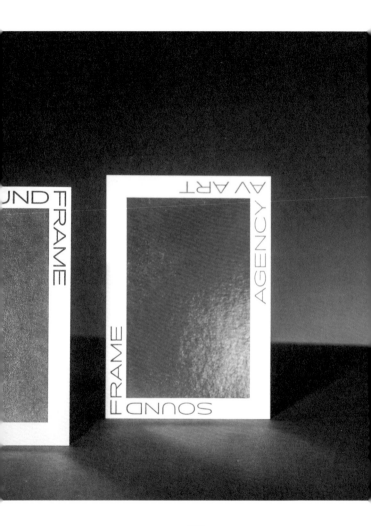

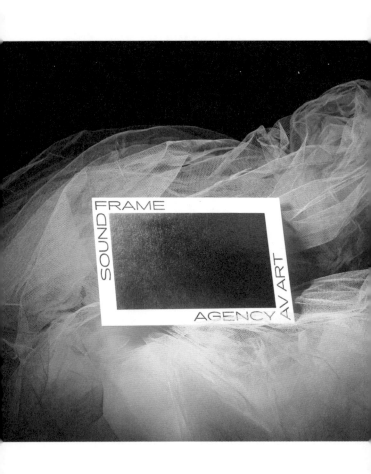

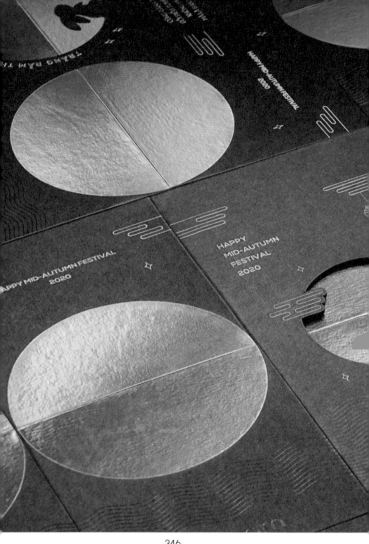

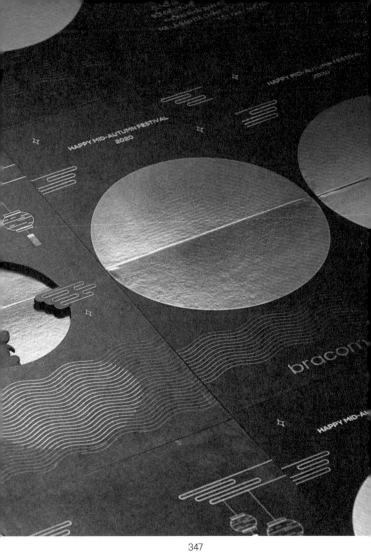

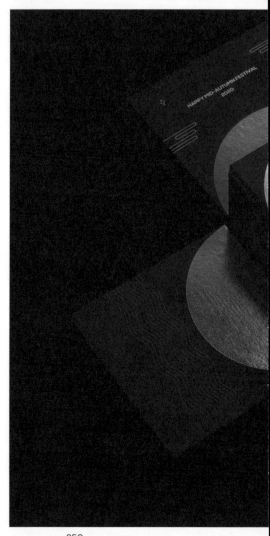

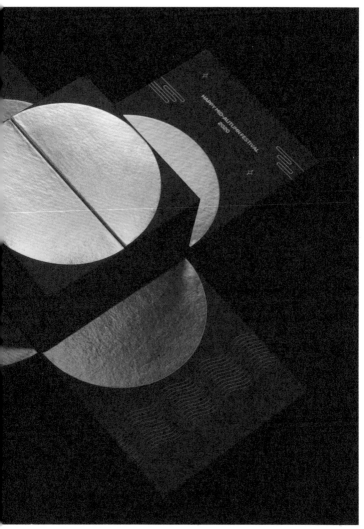

HAPPY MID-AUTUMN FESTIVAL
2020

THÉÂTRE ABC

LA CHAUX-DE-FONDS

SON : FRANCESCA MIZZONI
ET SARA PAPPALARDO
LUMIÈRES : JONAS BÜHLER

JE 30. 1181
VE 31 SA 02 2018
DI 26 1108

COPRODUCTION
PRODUCTION INTÉGRALE ET
CENTRE DE CULTURE ABC

RÉGIE : GASPARD MATILE
PRODUCTION : GABRIELA
DROGUETT FERNANDEZ

ABC-CULTURE.CH

THÉÂTRE A

SON : FRANCESCA MIZZONI
ET SARA PAPPALARDO
LUMIÈRES : JONAS BÜHLER

352

LA CHAUX-DE-FONDS

26—29 MARS 2015

ABC-CULTURE.CH

TEXTE
DIMITRIS DIMITRIADIS

MISE EN SCÈNE
ALIZA GRUBER

RÉGIE GASPARD MATILE
PRODUCTION DAMVILA
DRAGETT FERNANDEZ

YOUNG
BLACK
YOUTH

NIMA NABILI RAD
DIRECTOR
+61 (0) 403 203 8
NIMA@YBY.COM._
YBY.COM.AU

YOUNG
BLACK
YOUTH

NINA NABILI RAD
DIRECTOR
+61 (0) 403 203 845
NINA@YBI.COM.AU
YBI.COM.AU

NEXT TO THE OCEAN

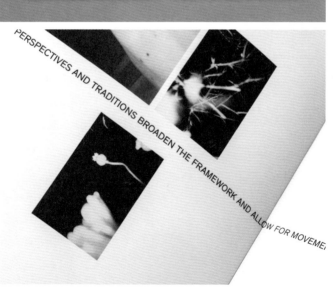

PERSPECTIVES AND TRADITIONS BROADEN THE FRAMEWORK AND ALLOW FOR MOVEMEN

Kamil Sipowicz

ENCYKLOPEDIA
POLSKIEJ
PSYCHODELII

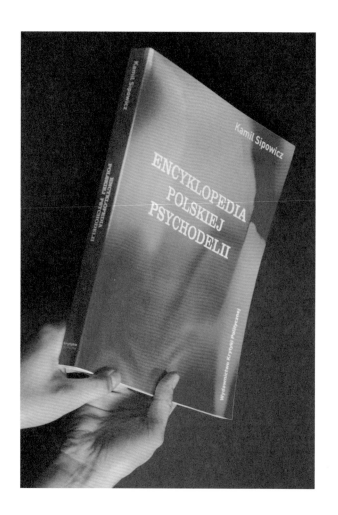

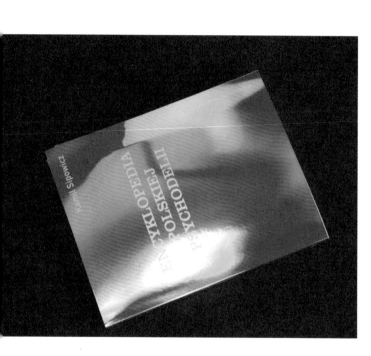

Kamil Sipowicz

ENCYKLOPEDIA
POLSKIEJ
PSYCHODELII

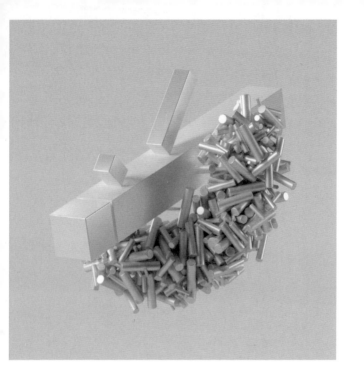

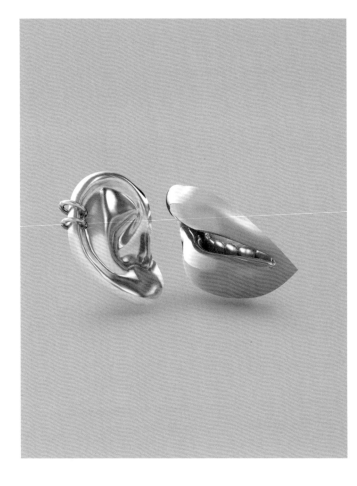

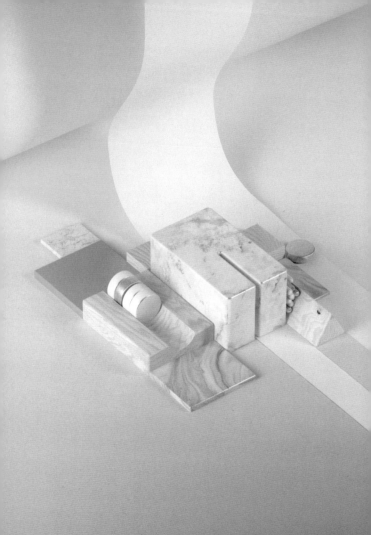

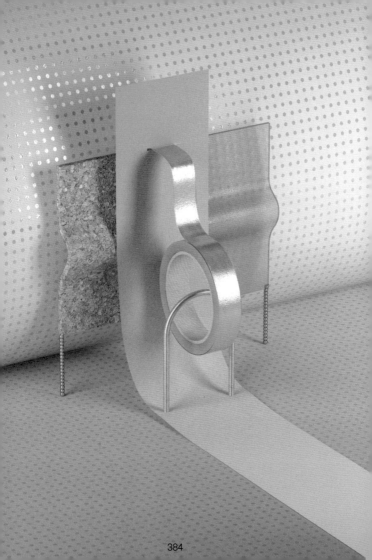

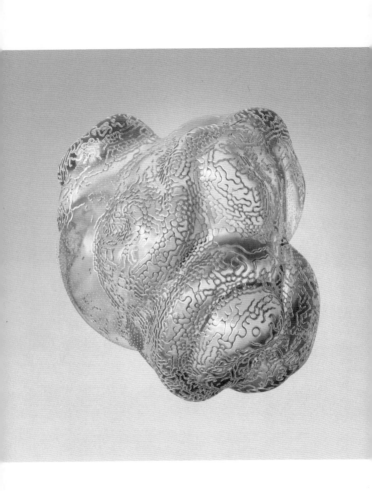

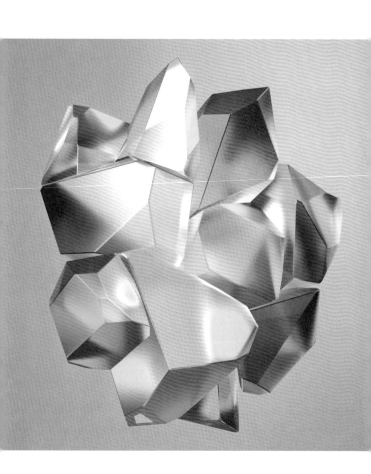

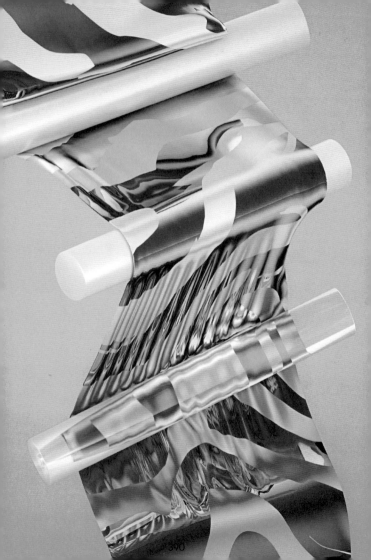

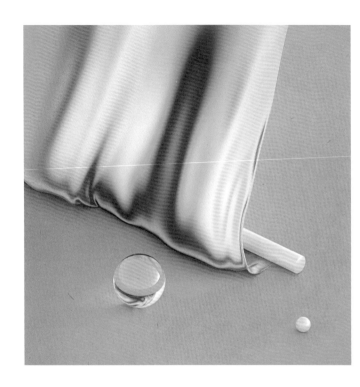

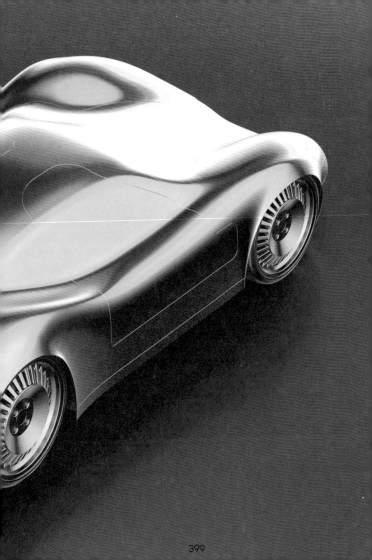

404

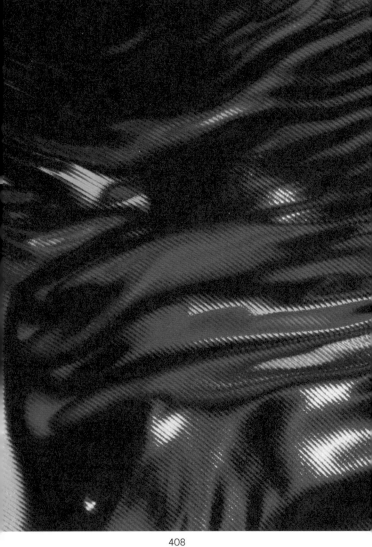

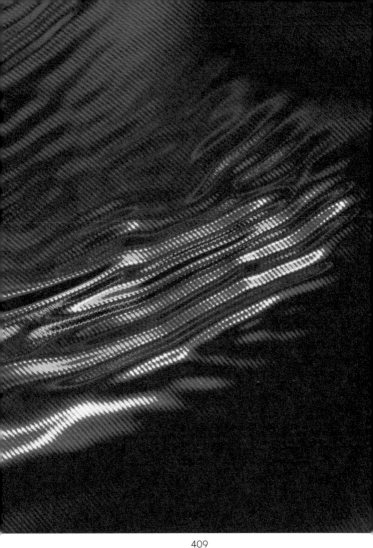

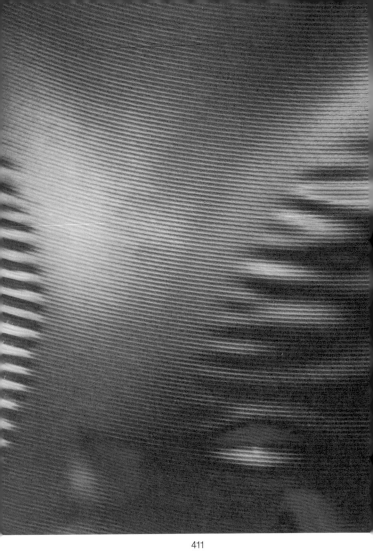

"Iridescence helped to enhance the magical and celebrational mood of the Strelka Closing Party. Seeing its brilliance, people knew that it was going to be an incredible night."

STRELKA
SUMMER
CLOSING
PARTY

MARK SCHEDRIN

16.09.17
22:00

INTERACTIVE PERFORMANCE

PSYCHE-
MAGIK
(UK)

#strelkasummer
strelka.com

CLOUD

JAMESON
IRISH WHISKEY

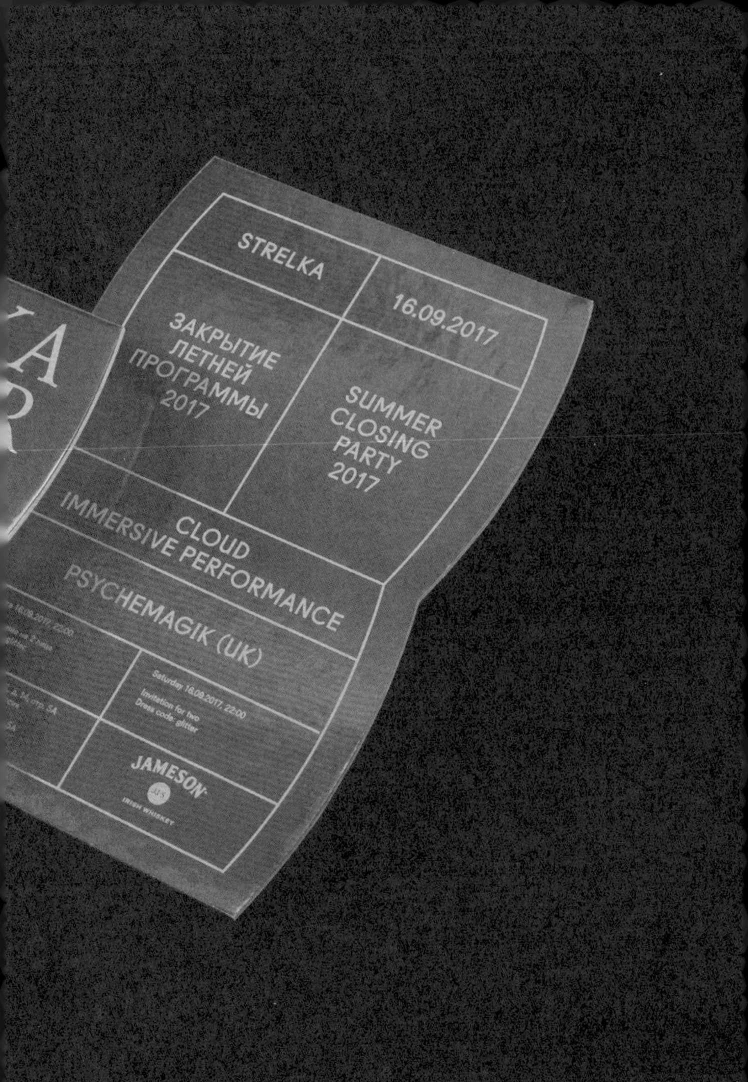

STRELKA

16.09.2017

ЗАКРЫТИЕ
ЛЕТНЕЙ
ПРОГРАММЫ
2017

SUMMER
CLOSING
PARTY
2017

CLOUD
IMMERSIVE PERFORMANCE

PSYCHEMAGIK (UK)

Saturday 16.09.2017, 22:00

Invitation for two
Dress code: glitter

JAMESON
IRISH WHISKEY

SIMIAN GHOST
The Veil

"Simian Ghost is by far one of Sweden's most interesting pop acts to come out this year"

noisey

"The result is a mature coming-together of all the band's practices with added sophistication and maturity"

The Telegraph

"The results are anything The band really met that sometimes feel like pop mellow"

CLASH

SIMIAN GHOST
The Veil

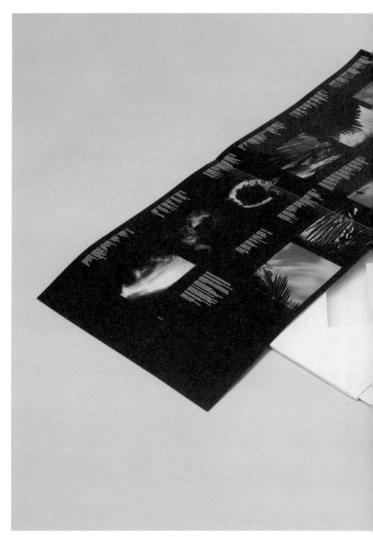

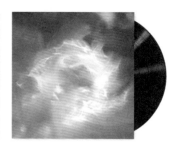

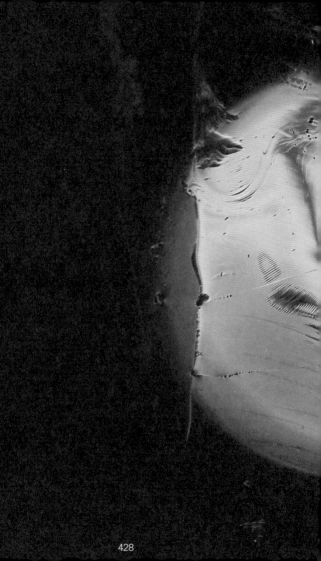

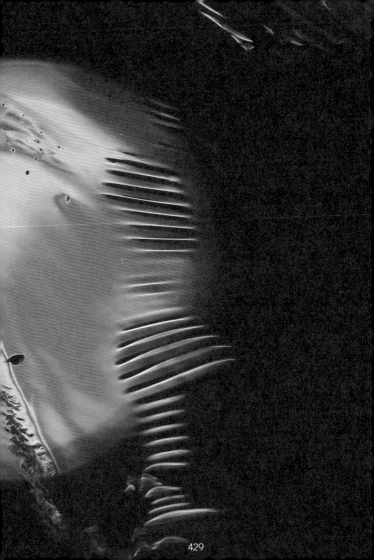

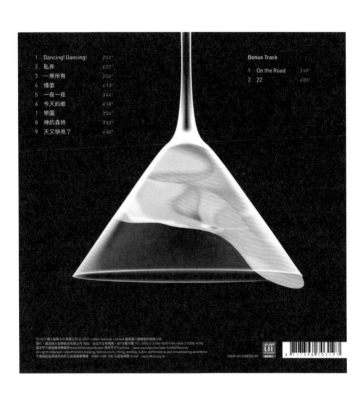

1　Dancing! Dancing!　2'51"
2　私奔　4'21"
3　一無所有　3'55"
4　情歌　4'13"
5　一夜一夜　3'44"
6　今天的歌　4'16"
7　樂園　3'24"
8　神的森林　3'45"
9　天又快亮了　4'40"

Bonus Track

1　On the Road　3'49"
2　22　4'03"

70319 4717398703197

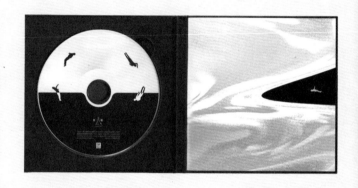

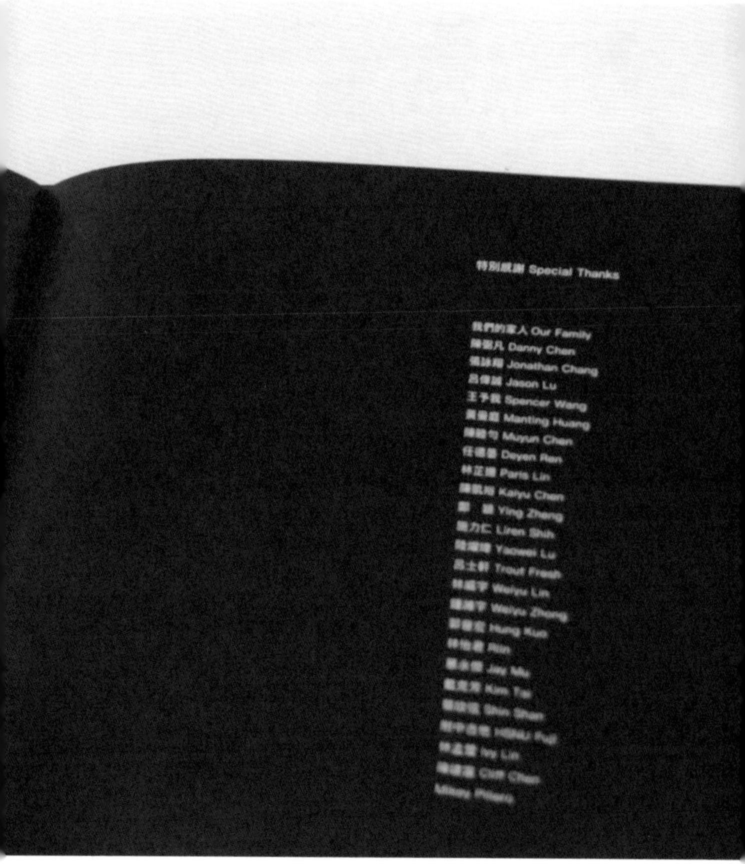

特別感謝 Special Thanks

我們的家人 Our Family
陳易凡 Danny Chen
張詠翔 Jonathan Chang
呂偉誠 Jason Lu
王宇毅 Spencer Wang
黃曼庭 Manting Huang
陳睦勻 Muyun Chen
任德彥 Deyen Ren
林芷緁 Paris Lin
陳凱裕 Kaiyu Chen
鄭 瑩 Ying Zhang
施力仁 Liren Shih
陸曜緯 Yaowei Lu
昌士軒 Trout Fresh
林維宇 Weiyu Lin
鍾維宇 Weiyu Zhong
郭竑宏 Hung Kuo
鈡怡 Riin
慕承樺 Jay Mu
戴克芳 Kim Tai
單幼珊 Shin Shan
許中吉格 HSRU Fuji
林孟璇 Ivy Lin
陳建廷 Cliff Chen
Mikey Pfeely

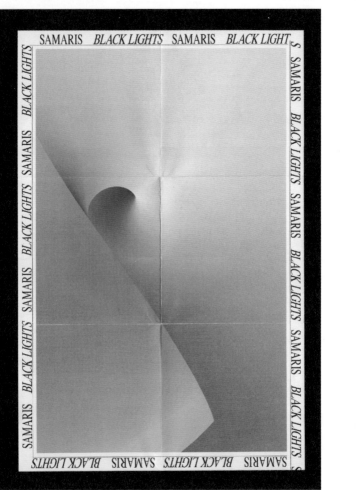

1 WANTED 2 SAY Heavy growth, harder life. Tread the water, or you die. It's the pressure of ours. Got the shore, got the wave. It's the only things we have. It's the treasure of ours. What is the point of making it right. This is the thing I wanted to say. What I wanted to say. Nothing at all. Pleasure is ours. **2 BLACK LIGHTS** White lights in the distance. Black lights when they close down. When the vaults open and the rain falls. Washes away the tar. But it won't undo. Come back to me. Attached to the thought impaired by the feeling. Nothing has carved as deep as you. Come back to me. Once more. All isn't gold when it's sunny. It's hard seeing things when you know you can't have any. It's hard to disguise when you want them to (find you). **3 GRADIENT SKY** Please be like you were back then. 'Cause I only know this one. 'Cause I don't know this one. Hard to grasp your slippery hands. Even if I want to. Please don't be like someone else. 'Cause I only want one. 'Cause I only know one. **4 T3MPO** I am speedy from the bottom of my heart. But with you I move no faster than you see. I can't feel your tempo. What is your tempo? Can you keep up with the driving force. Then fade into slow motion. Underwater. I can't feel your tempo. What is the matter? **5 I WILL** I thought I'd given you all. I thought there was nothing left. But now I know. I will. I thought you had taken my breath. I thought I was given yours. But now I know. I will. When you reach the point . I thought we carried the weight. I thought we made each other walk. **6 R4VIN** Days we sleep and hide at nightfall. With nerves more alert than ever. Darkness sheets cover every inch. We're blinded by glimpses of silver. We can chase the path. From the core to the stars. Shoot higher and hit harsher. With our back towards the sun. Never face what you run away from. Eyes are closed, no need to see straight. Dreams are more vivid than ever. It's a constant fight, it's a constant conquer. A journey that has no destination. **7 3Y3** I know what they say about it. I wish I'd relate to it. but I'm not one with it. Your eyes won't talk about it. It's not theirs to tell. (Their darkness stays dark). **8 T4NGLED** Your words got me tangled. Your whispers are soft as silk. Surround me with safety. You'll build me a fort. You always say. But the only thing that I hear. Is a siren shout. Run as quick as you can. Your arms were wide open, your grip on me strong. It's easy for you to think that you do. That you do it for me. No matter how you promise. And I want to believe you. The only thing I hear. Is a warning sign. Run as quick as you can. It's easy for you thinking. And saying you do. It makes the reality vanish from you. Your words tangled. And I don't know how. **9 IN DEEP** In deep is the place that unravels me. The easiest way to discomfort me. The tiniest breath unsettles me. Or sets me off. In deep is the current that controls me. The moon is constantly washing me over. Up high is the heaven that watches me. The mother is keeping an eye on me. Makes it so no one sets hands on me. Or sets me off.

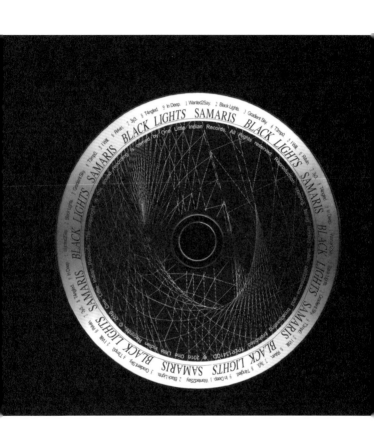

441

박근혜 - 최순실 게이트
관련 2차 대국민 사과에서

내가 이러려고 대통령을 했나라는
자괴감이 들정도로 괴롭기만 합니다

443

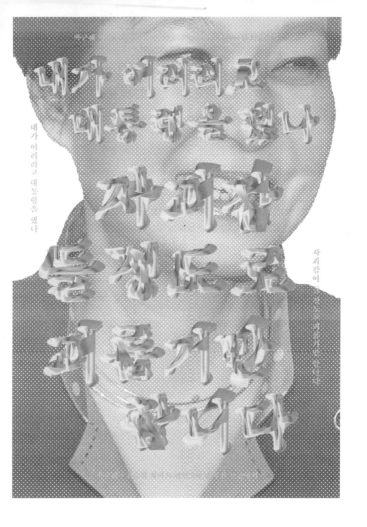

내가 이리로 대통령을 했나

자괴감이

444

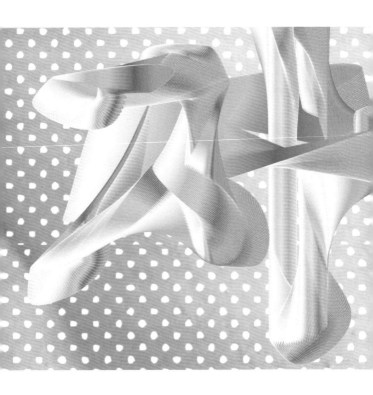

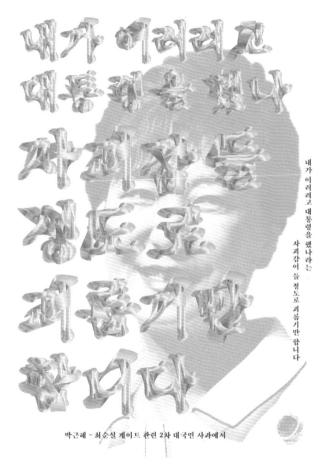

내가 이러려고
대통령을 했나

자괴감이 들고
정도로

괴롭기만
합니다

내가 이러려고 대통령을 했나라는 자괴감이 들 정도로 괴롭기만 합니다

박근혜 - 최순실 게이트 관련 2차 대국민 사과에서

Matías
Elichabehere

R h u m

Matías Elichabehere

Rhum

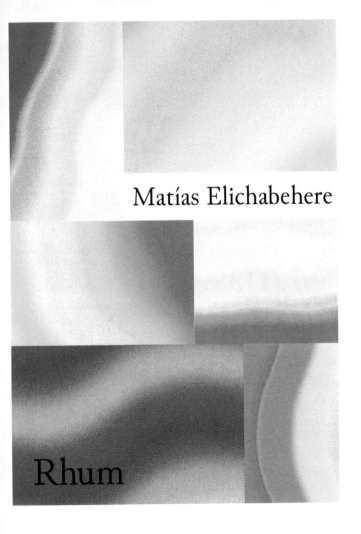

Matías Elichabehere

Rhum

450

Matías
Elichabehere

Rhum

UNDERSTAND RELATIONSHIP BETWEEN THINGS

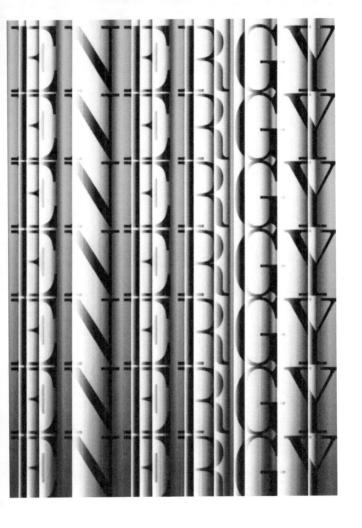

454

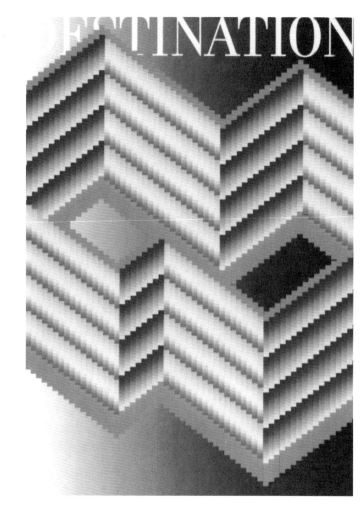

CONCENTRATION

Hey

Hey

461

Giorgia Zanellato.

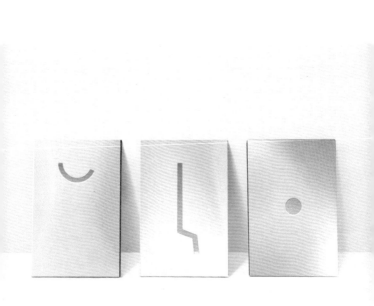

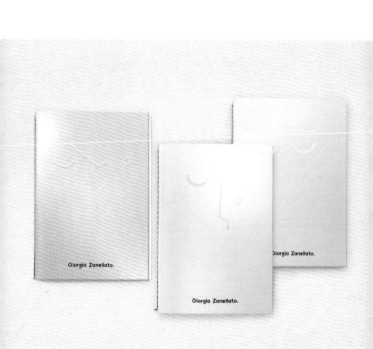

Giorgia Zanellato.

Giorgia Zanellato.

Giorgia Zanellato.

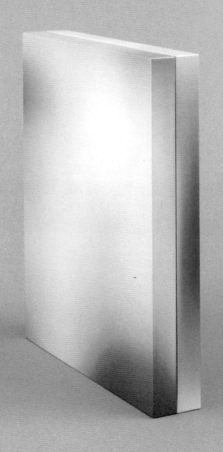

469

THE PEACOCK SOCIETY FESTIVAL

FESTIVAL DES CULTURES ÉLECTRONIQUES

WAREHOUSE VISUAL ARTS CLUB FILMS TALKS

VENDREDI **7** JUILLET 2017 SAMEDI **8**

PARC FLORAL DE PARIS | 22H > 7H

Nina Kraviz | Dixon | Kaytranada | Marcel Dettmann
Apollonia | The Martinez Brothers | The Black Madonna
Carl Craig PRESENTS VERSUS SYNTHESIZER ENSEMBLE | Jackmaster | Moodymann | Dvs1
Levon Vincent | Midland | Romare FULL LIVE BAND | Rejjie Snow
Tommy Genesis | Avalon Emerson | Konstantin
Jlin LIVE | Marie Davidson LIVE | Ancient Methods | Voiski LIVE | Azf
Peggy Gou | Fils De Venus | Raheem Experience (MAD REY, NEUE GRAFIK , LB AKA LABAT)
Hugo Lx | Varg LIVE | Blocaus w/ Exal | Blndr LIVE | Codex Empire LIVE
Kablam | Tgaf Crew | Bamao Yende (BOUKAN REC) | Oko Dj

INFOS & PRÉVENTES SUR THEPEACOCKSOCIETY.FR

#NEEDTODANCE

FESTIVAL DES CULTURES ÉLECTRONIQUES

WAREHOUSE VISUAL ARTS CLUB FILMS TALKS

VENDREDI **7** JUILLET 2017 SAMEDI **8**

"Iridescent colours and the structures that produce them have unique properties. It is interesting to have colour distortions in design."

cycladic

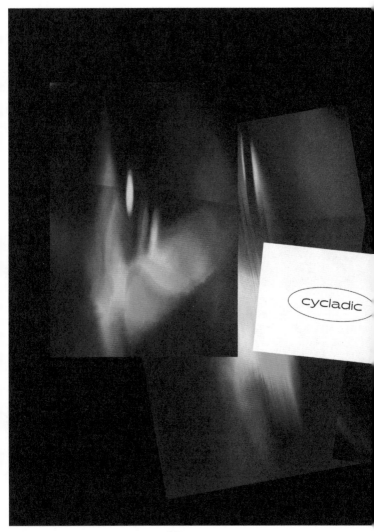

cycladic

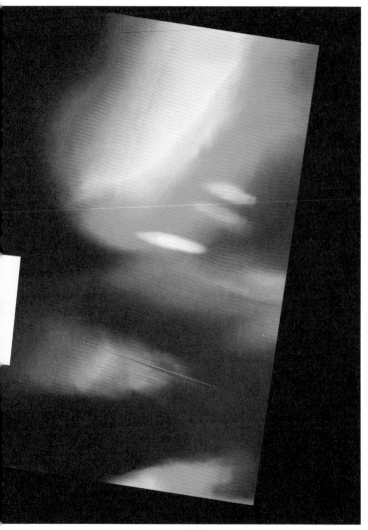

NORTH AMERICA TOUR
03/18
Seattle, WA

NORTH AMERICA TOUR
03/22
Los Angeles, CA

NORTH AMERICA TOUR
03/27
Washington, DC

NORTH AMERICA TOUR
04/07
Brooklyn, NY

EUROPE SPRING TOUR
03/06
Krakow, Poland

EUROPE SPRING TOUR
03/08
Warsaw, Poland

NORTH AMERICA TOUR
04/11
Vancouver, BC

NORTH AMERICA TOUR
04/16
Edmonton, AB

NORTH AMERICA TOUR
05/06
Atlanta, GA

NORTH AMERICA TOUR
05/10
Denver, CO

EUROPE TOUR
18/06
Amsterdam, Netherlands

EUROPE TOUR
22/06
Milan, Italy

NORTH AMERICA TOUR
05/01
Dallas, TX

NORTH AMERICA TOUR
05/05
Houston, TX

EUROPE TOUR
13/07
Paris, France

EUROPE TOUR
16/07
London, England

NORTH AMERICA TOUR 2018
for more information www.cycladic.com

cycladic

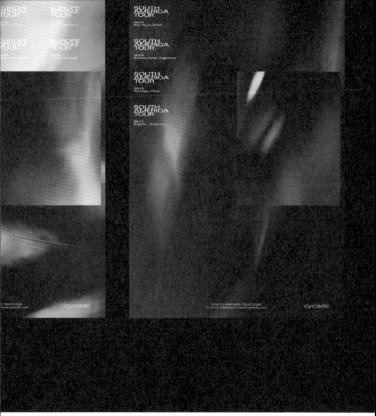

NORTH AMERICA TOUR

2/16
Seattle, WA

NORTH AMERICA TOUR

02/20
Los Angeles, CA

NORTH AMERICA TOUR

03/27
Washington, DC

NORTH AMERICA TOUR

4/11
Vancouver, BC

NORTH AMERICA TOUR

04/28
Edmonton, AB

NORTH AMERICA TOUR

05/05
Atlanta, GA

NORTH AMERICA TOUR

05/21
Dallas, TX

NORTH AMERICA TOUR

05/25
Houston, TX

ORTH
MERICA
OUR

7
oklyn, NY

ORTH
MERICA
OUR

0
ver, CO

EUROPE
SPRING
TOUR

1/06
rakow, Poland

EUROPE
SPRING
TOUR

02/06
Warsaw, Poland

EUROPE
SPRING
TOUR

06/06
Vienna, Austria

EUROPE
SPRING
TOUR

3/06
msterdam, Netherlands

EUROPE
SPRING
TOUR

22/06
Milan, Italy

EUROPE
SPRING
TOUR

23/06
Barcelona, Spain

EUROPE
SPRING
TOUR

3/07
aris, France

EUROPE
SPRING
TOUR

16/07
London, England

Hey	Hey	Hey
Eva Vesikansa Senior Designer & Art Director Pallars 141, 3B 08018 Barcelona +34 936 762 400 eva@heystudio.es	Gemma Fajardo HeyShop Manager Pallars 141, 3B 08018 Barcelona +34 936 762 400 gemma@heystudio.es	Verònica Fuerte Founder & Creativ Palla 080 +34 vero
Hey	Hey	Hey
Eva Vesikansa Senior Designer & Art Director Pallars 141, 3B 08018 Barcelona +34 936 762 400 eva@heystudio.es	Verònica Fuerte Founder & Creative Director Pallars 141, 3B 08018 Barcelona +34 936 762 400 veronica@heystudio.es	Adrià Molins Designer Pal 080 +3 adr
Hey	Hey	Hey
Verònica Fuerte Founder & Creative Director Pallars 141, 3B 08018 Barcelona +34 936 762 400 veronica@heystudio.es	Verònica Fuerte Founder & Creative Director Pallars 141, 3B 08018 Barcelona +34 936 762 400 veronica@heystudio.es	Eva Vesikansa Senior Designer & Pa 08 +3 eva
Hey	Hey	Hey
Eva Vesikansa Senior Designer & Art Director Pallars 141, 3B 08018 Barcelona +34 936 762 400 eva@heystudio.es	Eva Vesikansa Senior Designer & Art Director Pallars 141, 3B 08018 Barcelona +34 936 762 400 eva@heystudio.es	Adrià Molins Designer Pa 08 +3 ad
Hey	Hey	Hey
Eva Vesikansa Senior Designer & Art Director Pallars 141, 3B 08018 Barcelona +34 936 762 400 eva@heystudio.es	Gemma Fajardo HeyShop Manager Pallars 141, 3B 08018 Barcelona +34 936 762 400 gemma@heystudio.es	Paula Sánchez Project Manager Pa 08 +3 pa

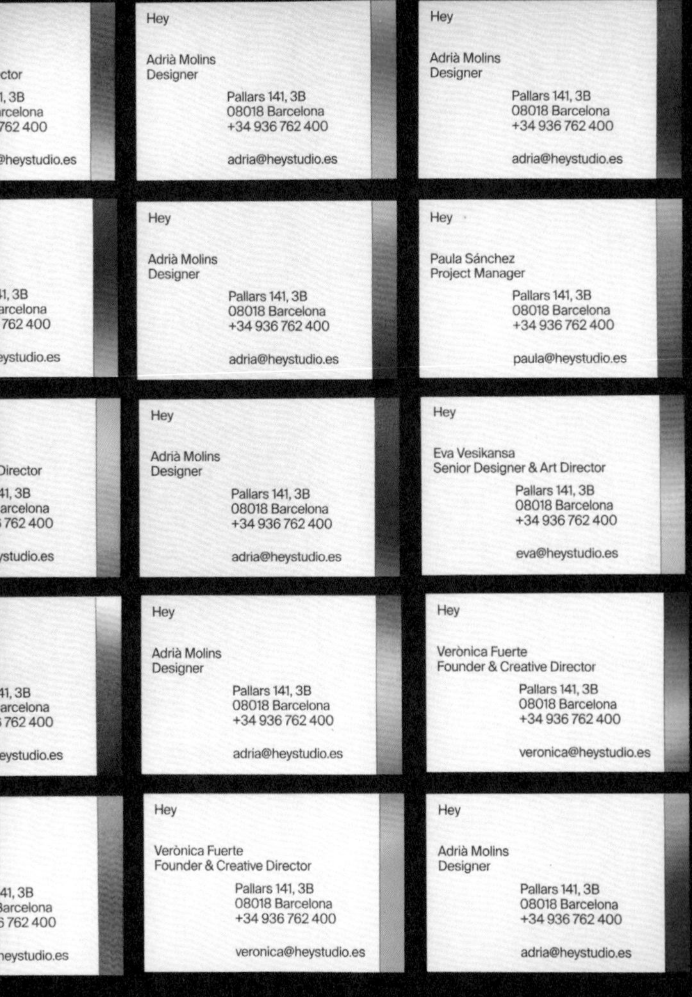

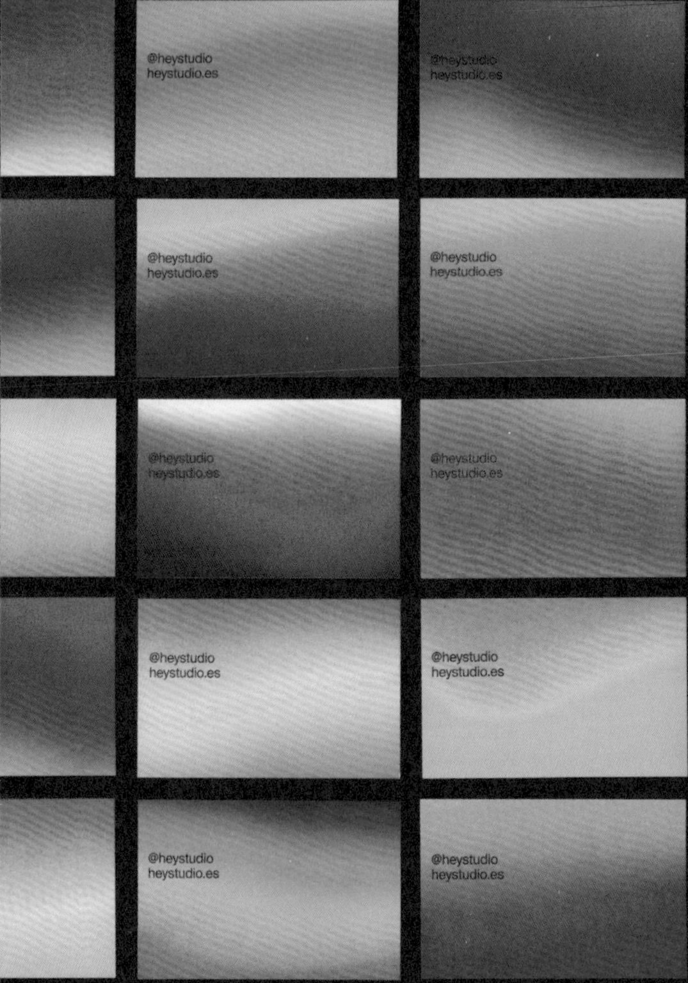

Adrià Molins
Designer

Pallars 141, 3B
08018 Barcelona
+34 936 762 400

adria@heystudio.es

Hey

Adrià Molins
Designer

Pallars 141, 3B
08018 Barcelona
+34 936 762 400

adria@heystudio.es

Hey

Adrià Molins
Designer

Pallars 141, 3B
08018 Barcelona
+34 936 762 400

adria@heystudio.es

Hey

Gemma Fa
HeyShop Mar

P
08
+34

gemma@

SAM —FOX LECTURE SERIES 2016 ____

CALENDAR OF EVENTS

SEPT—DEC

FILM SCREENINGS AND EXHIBITIONS

DISCUSSIONS AND WORKSHOPS

WASHINGTON UNIVERSTIY IN ST. LOUIS

9.09
Museum Exhibition Opening & 10th Anniversary Celebration
Real / Radical / Psychological
The Collection on Display
6–10p | Gallery, Kemper Art Museum

9.10
Gallery Talk
Sabine Eckmann
1p | Kemper Art Museum

9.14
Artist Talk & Book Signing
Charlie le Mindu
6–8p | Ferry Auditorium

9.15
Spotlight Talk
Allison Unruh
5p | Kemper Art Museum

9.19
Public Lecture Series
Dario Robleto
6p Reception | 6:30p Lecture – Steinberg
Steinberg Auditorium

9.21
Discussions in Architectural History and Theory Lecture
Robin Middleton
6pm | Steinberg Auditorium

9.23
Film Screening
Free Cities: Spawning the Future
6p | Steinberg Auditorium

9.26
Public Lecture Series
Martino Stierli
6p Reception | Kemper Art Museum
6:30p Lecture | Steinberg Auditorium

9.27
Dedication of the Douglas B. Dowd Modern Graphic History Library
10a–Noon Open House | Weil Campus
3–4p Symposium | Brown Hall
4p Reception, 4:30p Lecture | Steinberg Auditorium

Thinking the Museums: Exhibition Design
Sabine Eckmann, Frank Escher, Ravi GuneWardena, Angela Pang, & Jan Ulmer
6p | Kemper Art Museum

9.28
Public Lecture Series
Wangechi Mutu
6p Reception | 6:30p Lecture

10.4
Kemper Art Museum Film Series
Pollock (2000)
7p | Brodt Theatre, 6330 Delmar Blvd.

10.5
Kemper Art Museum Film Series
Moulin Rouge (1952)
7p | Brodt Theatre, 6330 Delmar Blvd.

10.6
Kemper Art Museum Film Series
The Mystery of Picasso (1956)
7p | Brodt Theatre, 6330 Delmar Blvd.

10.6
Kemper Art Museum Film Series
The Mystery of Picasso (1956)
7p | Tivoli Theatre, 6350 Delmar Blvd.

10.7
Opening Reception
Ontology of Influence: Ron Leax and Alumni Exhibition
6–9p | Des Lee Gallery, 1627 Washington Ave.

10.13
Spotlight Talk
Elizabeth C. Childs
5p | Kemper Art Museum

10.19
Public Lecture Series
Shelley Rice
6p Reception | Kemper Art Museum
6:30p Lecture | Steinberg Auditorium

10.20
Public Lecture Series
Amale Andraos
6p Reception | 6:30p Lecture Steinberg Auditorium

10.21
Informal Chin Workshop Lecture
Amale Andraos
6p Reception | 6:30p Lecture Steinberg Auditorium

10.24
Performance
Art Inspiring Music: New Morse Code
7p | Kemper Art Museum

10.24
Public Lecture Series
Seymour Chwast
6p Reception | 6:30p Lecture, Steinberg Auditorium

10.24
Public Lecture Series
Seymour Chwast
6p Reception | 6:30p Lecture, Steinberg Auditorium

10.27
Gallery Talk
Allison Unruh
1p | Kemper Art Museum

10.29
Family Fun Saturday
11a–2p | Kemper Art Museum

11.7
Public Lecture Series
Tom Friedman
6p Reception | Kemper Art Museum
6:30p Lecture | Steinberg Auditorium

11.9
Public Lecture Series
Philippe Rahm
6p Reception | 6:30p Lecture Steinberg Auditorium

11.14
Public Lecture Series
Meredith Malone
6p | Kemper Art Museum

11.14
Public Lecture Series
Henry L. and Natalie E. Freund Visiting Artist Lecture
6p Reception | 6:30p Lecture Steinberg Auditorium

12.1
Spotlight Talk
Jennifer Padgett
5p | Kemper Art Museum

12.2
Opening Reception
Parabola 2016
6–8p | Des Lee Gallery, 1627 Washington Ave.

497

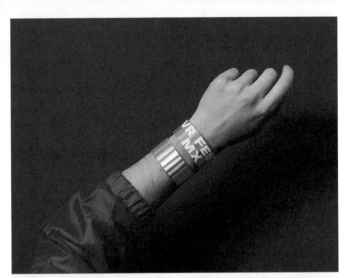

500

LONDON
FASHION
WEEK
15-19 SEPTEMBER 2017

Welcome to London Fashion Week

LONDON FASHION WEEK
15-19 SEPTEMBER 2017

The British Fashion Council
invites you to

Date

Time

505

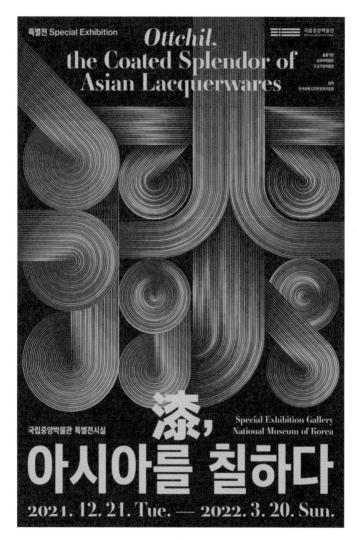

특별전 Special Exhibition

Ottchil,
the Coated Splendor of
Asian Lacquerwares

국립중앙박물관
NATIONAL MUSEUM OF KOREA

국립중앙박물관 특별전시실

漆,
아시아를 칠하다

Special Exhibition Gallery
National Museum of Korea

2021. 12. 21. Tue. — 2022. 3. 20. Sun.

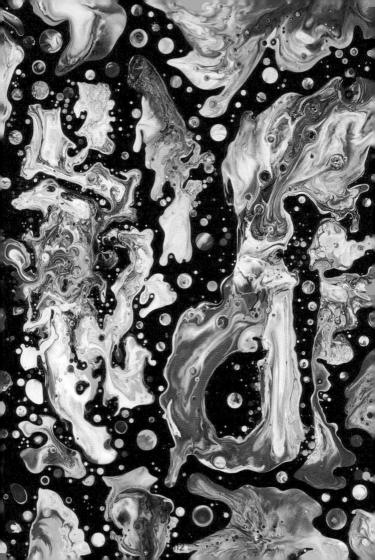

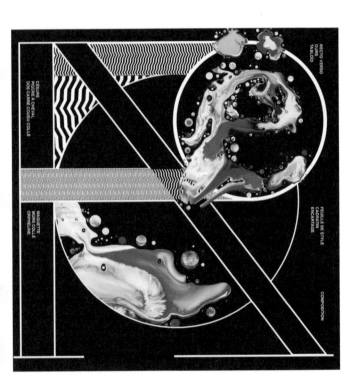

CESURA
PIQÛRE À CHEVAL
KANSIPAPÍR

GOUTTIÈRE
ΑΠΡΟΨ
INSGUARDI

RECTO VERSO
SCHUTBLAD

BUCHFORMAT
EM DASH
スタイルシート

ШМУЦТИТУЛ
페이지 레이아웃
CHEMIN DE FER

COMPOSITION

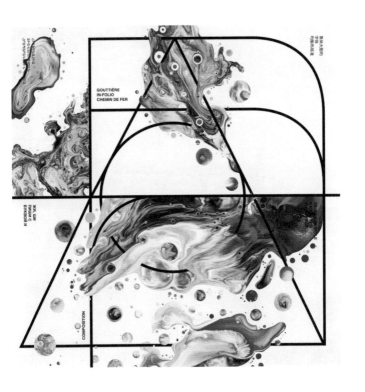

GOUTTIÈRE
IN-FOLIO
CHEMIN DE FER

COMPOSITION

ЖК ШИ
ПИШИ С
БУКВОЙ И

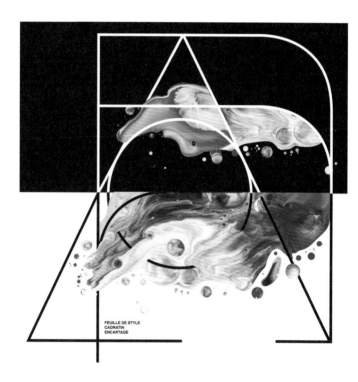

FEUILLE DE STYLE
CADRATIN
ENCARTAGE

DESIGN

ADOBE

ADOBE

DESIGN

This exhibition is a conceptual representation of heat in its most immediate expression, temperature.

A guided experience through a series of artistic and sensory installations which "give shape" to one the most widely used means to transfer heat. This gallery of multi-cultural creative visions is conceived by the international team of young designers at Fabrica for Daikin, a firm that has always been committed to provide the "climate for life", promoting the responsible use of energy harmony with nature. the domestic environment this becomes design thanks to Emura.

MIGRATION
A SERIES OF KINETIC
SCULPTURES DEPICTS THE
FLOCKING PATTERNS OF
MIGRATING BIRDS AS THEY
MOVE BETWEEN HOT & COLD
CLIMATES. THE 6 EXHIBITS
FEATURE MOTORISED, HAND
ILLUSTRATED FEATHERS TO
COMMUNICATE THE RITUALS
OF EACH BIRD SPECIES,
CHARACTERISED BY HEIGHT,
DISTANCE AND FLOCK SIZE
DURING FLIGHT.

32"

3

BRAIN
NETWORKS

4

TECHNICAL
NETWORKS

"Iridescence
as a means of
communication
is far older than
humanity."

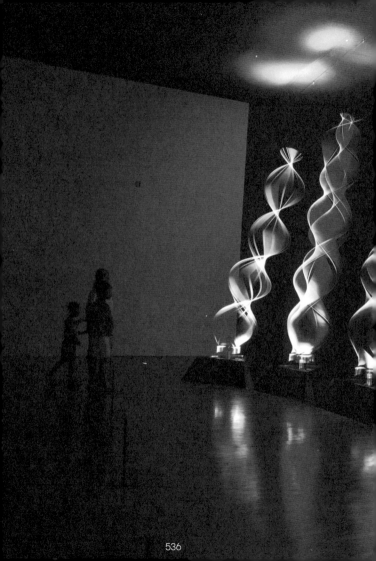

festival techno audiovisual

25___27
/11 / 16

Ciudad Cultural Konex

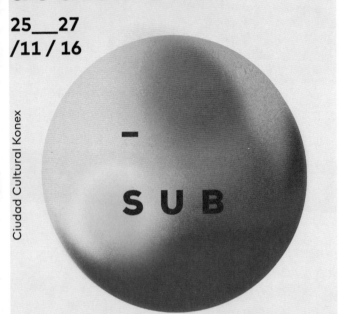

—
S U B

festival techno
audiovisual

PRIMER
DE PRODUCCIÓN MUSICAL
CON ABLETON 9.7
SEMINARIO

27/11 - 22 hs.
Sala B

/ dj / productores / principiantes / aficionados

SUB

Ciudad
Cultural
Konex

PRIMER
DE PRODUCCIÓN MUSICAL
CON ABLETON 9.7
27/11 - 22 hs.
Sala B
SEMINARIO

/ dj / productores / principiantes / aficionados

SUB
Festival
Techno
Audiovisual

27 / 11
22.00 hs.
Sala B

de música electrónica

seminario con ableton

En el marco de acercar
la música electrónica a
los jóvenes y curiosos,
enseñándoles lo que
involucra el trabajo del
productor, las máquinas,
y el uso integral de las
aplicaciones relaciona-
das con la producción,
mostrando en forma
clara y dinámica el
quehacer del músico
electrónico, generando
un ambiente donde los
participantes vean a los
artistas en acción y
puedan interactuar con
esta nueva forma de
expresión musical.

Descubre la tecnología
detrás del último
lanzamiento de ABLE-
TON, el controlador
ABLETON PUSH y la
nueva versión ABLETON
LIVE 9. Jaison Sosa te
mostrará las nuevas
funciones y ventajas que
ofrece esta para que
tus producciones
sean únicas.

dictado por:

Carlos Alfonsín y
Johann Kopp

TALLER DE PRODUCCIÓN DE MÚSICA

SUB Festival Techno Audiovisual

/ grabación / edición / mezcla / síntesis / mezclador virtual / transformación en tiempo real / secuenciación / instrumentos virtuales / realización de una canción / mezcla / postproducción / teoría del sonido / microfonía y grabación / editores de audio / secuenciadores / sampleador virtual / aproximación a Reason / Ableton y reverse / edición

ELECTRÓNICA / MEZCLA

25 / 11
18.00 hs.
Sala B

Y ARTE SONORO

TALLER DE PRODUCCIÓN DE MÚSICA ELECTRÓNICA MEZCLA Y ARTE SONORO

Sala B
18.00 hs.
25 / 11

SUB Festival Techno Audiovisual

25 / 11
18.00 hs.
Sala B

/ grabación / edición /
mezcla / síntesis /
/ mezclador virtual /
transformación en tiempo
real / secuenciación /
instrumentos virtuales /
realización de una canción /
mezcla / postproducción /
teoría del sonido / microfonía y grabación / editores
de audio / secuenciadores /
sampleador virtual /
aproximación a Reason y
Ableton / edición, uso de
maestros y loops

dirigido a:

/ músicos / ingenieros /
artistas sonoros y visuales
/ informáticos, y en
general, / todos aquellos
interesados en el mundo
de la música electrónica
y el audio digital y
masterización

dictado por:

Carlos Alfonsín y
John200 Kopp

oscuridad del
onido/
sonido de la
scuridad/
movimiento a través
el sonido/ el sonido a
avés de la imagen /
imagen en
ovimiento/
movimiemto a
avés de la imagen

narios

+ de 100 artistas

2 escenarios principales

5 salas de exposición

3 shows 3d

ones

/ djs

/ Detroit /
Barcelona / Ibiza /
Buenos Aires

TECHNO

/ AUDIOVISUAL

Londres / Praga
/ Brujas / Berlín

/conferencias

Mischa / Post Scrip-
tum / Skee Mask T.
Linder / Refracted /
Iraeli [uy] / Deepcho
Max Hill / Mix [hntz]
Headlind / Tarcar /
HeadlindKbull /
Ratbad / Scotch Eg
/ Skratch+Orson /
Sleeparchive / Andre
Zacco / Oreene /
Talker / Mark Verbos
Regus / Peder +Par
/Fraw / Pur / Jeal
Party / John Collins
Moritz Von Oswald
Ryan Kansek / Fit-
Siegel / Po Sounds /
Tapes / Dynamo /
Felix / Abdula R /
Skarn [live] / Shiftec
Sigma Out LR Willi
Turns / Anton / Marl
Redder Ena / Ooth
Rad / Presha

internationaal
podiumkunsten
amsterdam
juni 2017

70 jaar
holland festival
bestel nu kaarten
hollandfestival.nl

HOLLAND
FESTIVAL

FONDS 21

A
O   M
D
   O
M

Rabobank

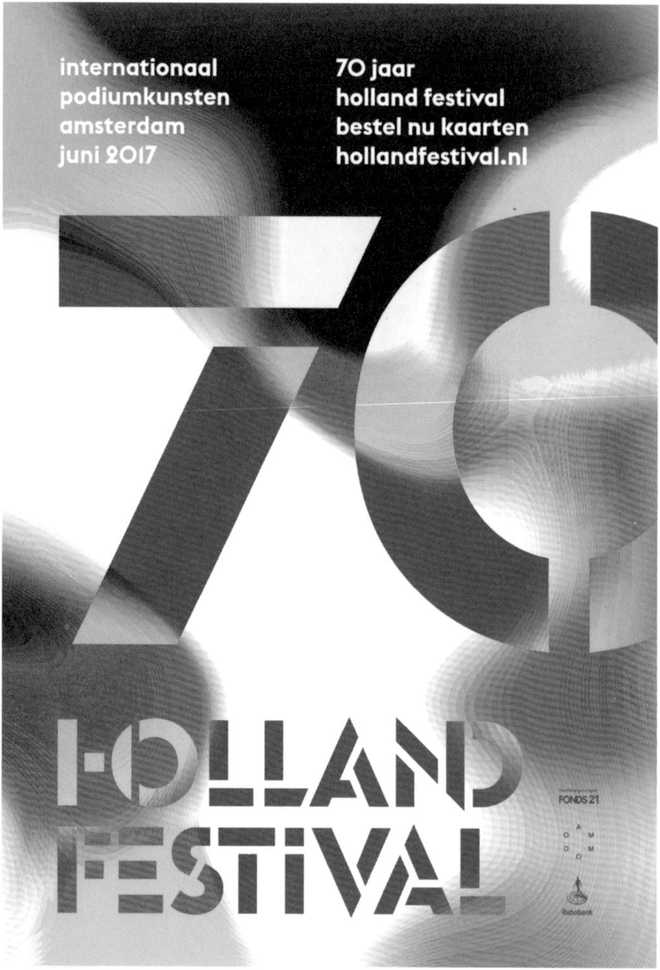

internationaal
podiumkunsten
amsterdam
juni 2017

70 jaar
holland festival
bestel nu kaarten
hollandfestival.nl

HOLLAND
FESTIVAL

FONDS 21

Rabobank

onaal
nsten
am

70

AR

"I love to imagine that the consciousness, dreams, thoughts, and ideas within us are materialised by iridescence."

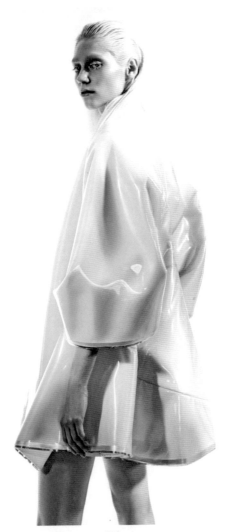

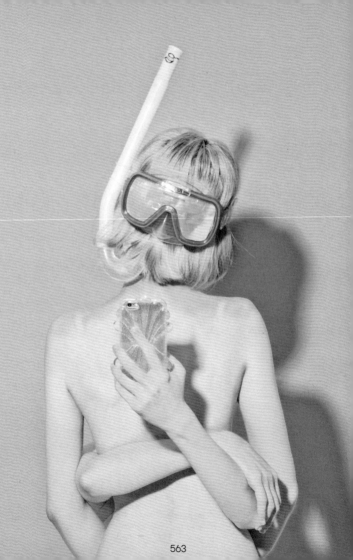

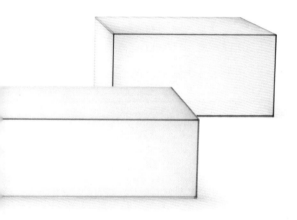

"Colours are very powerful communica-tion tools for people around the world, with-out the need for words."

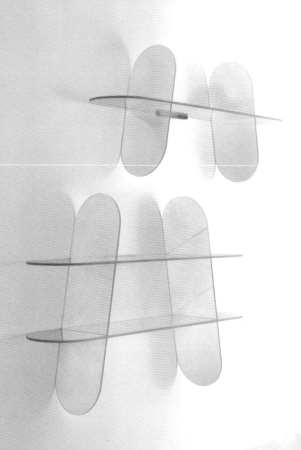

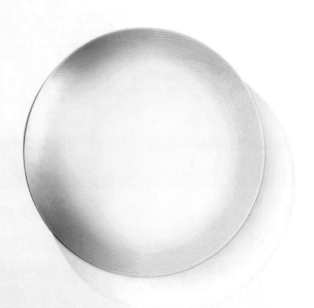

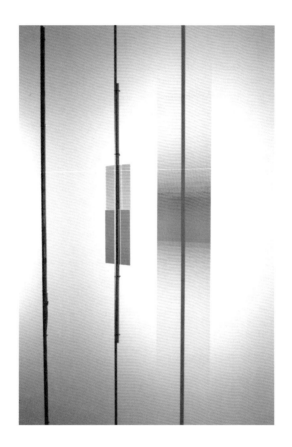

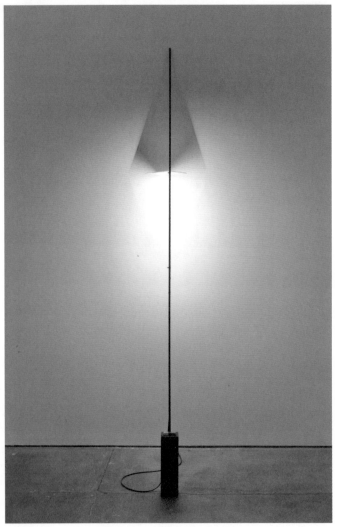

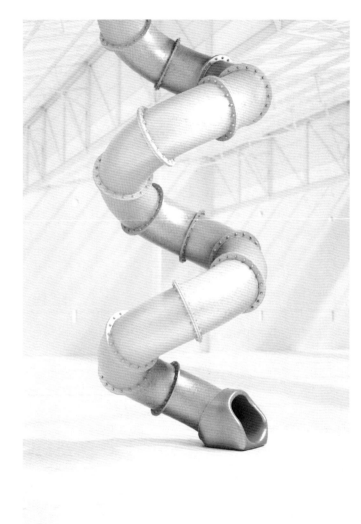

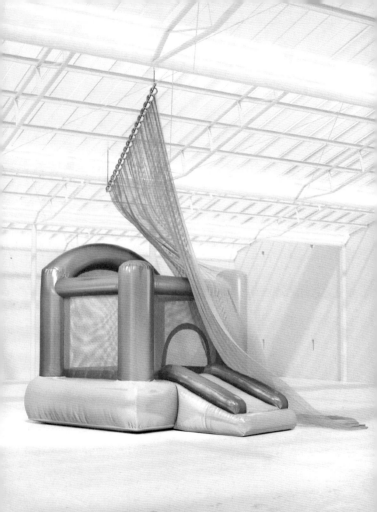

609

INDEX

BIOGRAPHY

101

101.at

101 is a coding and design agency that believes in the power of a good concept. They work with, and not for, their clients, as they are convinced that in meeting eye-to-eye, the best results can be achieved. By seeking challenges in every project, they aim to surprise their clients and themselves with ideas and solutions.

PP. 342–345

Aaron Nieh

aaronnieh.com

Since the last decade, Aaron Nieh Workshop has been leading influence in the fields of pop music, culture, theatre, and branding through its provocative, ambitious and imaginative design presentation.

PP. 182–187

Alexia Roux

alexiaroux.fr

Alexia is a graphic designer based in Montpellier. She designs visual identities for various types of projects, including branding and publishing. Her skills lie in art direction as well as print and web design, where she attaches particular importance to the uniqueness of a brand image.

PP. 162–165, 202–205

Alexis Jamet

alecsi.com

Alexis is a French graphic designer whose diverse work ranges from conventional identities to bright and charming illustrations. He shares his time between graphic design, art direction, and drawing.

PP. 448–451

Alycia Rainaud

alyciarainaud.com

Alycia is a French graphic designer based in Marseille. Influenced and driven by publishing and hybrid books, she has also started working as a digital artist known as Malavida to experiment with new technologies, digital painting, programming, and visual effects.

PP. 242–245

Amanda Reiter

amandareiter.com

Amanda is a graphic designer whose approach is rooted in visual research and conceptual thinking. With a background in neuroscience and psychology, she wishes to use design to shape meaningful human experiences for her audiences. She focuses on branding, illustration, packaging, art direction and everything in between.

PP. 494–495

Anagrama

anagrama.com

Anagrama is an international branding firm specialising in the design of brands, objects, spaces, software and multi-media. It thrives on breaking the traditional creative agency scheme, integrating multidisciplinary teams of creative and business experts.

ANDON DESIGN DAILY CO., LTD

andondesigndaily.com

&ON is a collective of passionate designers who use design to bring the true value of experiences to life. Through various inventive experiments, &ON delves deep into the fundamentals of design in order to craft the best brand that lasts by collaborating closely with their clients.

Anna Kulachek

kulachek.com

Anna is a Ukrainian graphic designer. After her residency at Fabrica in Treviso, she became an art director at the Strelka Institute for Media, Architecture and Design, where she currently oversees all the visualisation of public and educational programmes. She also works for the Strelka Press, a publishing house at the Institute.

Aron Tzimas

arontzimas.com

Aron is a New York-based designer working on everything from UI/UX app design to restaurant design and branding. Originally from Melbourne, he has founded many projects around the world and is currently the Chief Creative Officer of Knotch Inc.

PP. 108–113

Balmer Hählen

balmerhahlen.ch

Balmer Hählen was founded in 2011 by Priscilla Balmer and Yvo Hählen. Currently based in Lausanne, they are involved in various collaborative projects with designers, stylists, artists, photographers, and printers. They pay special attention to the quality of their prints for outstanding outcomes.

PP. 280–281

Barmaleys Studio

barmaleys.studio

Specialising in food and restaurant identites, Barmaleys Studio has a rich portfolio to show for its expertise. They also has a great appetite for new and bold projects, aiming to create not only stylish and conventient solutions, but also practical tools based on brand-strategy.

PP. 266–269

BLOW

blow.hk

BLOW is a Hong Kong-based design studio founded by Ken Lo in 2010. They specialise in branding, packaging, print, and website design. As part of their creative ethos, they provide clients with simple and inspiring work powered by great ideas and executed with a high level of craftsmanship.

PP. 212–221

bonjour garçon studio

bonjourgarcon.fr

bonjour garçon studio is a Paris-based creative studio that was founded by Romain Fritiau and Pierre Tostain, a graphic designer and photographer respectively. Their works often embody their vision of the contemporary landscape through creative direction, graphic design, print, editorials, and fashion photography.

PP. 476–483

BRACOM AGENCY

bracom.agency

Based in Saigon, Bracom is a full-service branding and packaging agency. With a young and dynamic team, Bracom delivers brand stories in an authentic and unique manner, and has claimed numerous awards including Dieline Awards, Muse Creative Awards, PRINT Awards, and more.

PP. 258–265, 346–351

Bruce Mau Design

brucemaudesign.com

Bruce Mau Design brands organisations that are shaping the future of their respective industries worldwide. Their passion lies in bringing compelling ideas to life, invigorating brands, and helping businesses grow. Their creative work is recognised for its depth of thought, clarity of purpose, and boldness of vision.

PP. 192–195

Build

studio.build

Build is an award-winning creative studio with an international reputation for creating strong visual narratives. Utilising art direction and graphic design, they create brand identities, websites, packaging, and books for design-led clients around the world.

PP. 206–211

By Electra

byelectra.com

Adriana Mora is a Mexican designer, digital illustrator, 3D artist and branding designer. She leads as a 3D generalist and art director at ByElectra, an ongoing collaboration of designers. She has also developed campaigns for clients including Apple, Adidas, Uber, Microsoft and many more.

PP. 604–607

Caroline Blanchette

behance.net/carolineblanchette

Caroline is an award-winning graphic designer and art director. She has worked with multiple international advertising agencies for leading brands from all over the world.

PP. 170–175

Catello Gragnaniello

behance.net/catelloo

Catello was born in Naples, where he currently lives and works. Driven by his passion for technology, he began dabbling in 3D graphics and motion graphic design after bouts of experimentation. His recent work is the result of exploring new perspectives and means of expression.

PP. 371–375

Chiii Design

chiiidesign.com

Chiii Design specialises in integrating commercial elements with arts and culture. Headquartered in Macau, the studio provides consultancy services that focus on brand image and packaging design. Through their international vision and unique style, they are making waves in Asia, the U.K., the U.S. and beyond.

PP. 500–503

Chulwoong Lee

behance.net/wooongtone

Chulwoong has a master's degree in communication design from Kookmin University. He seeks design expressions that extend beyond the two-dimensional. His interest in abstractness, fortuity, and infinity rather than delivering a clear message drives him to explore the true role of a designer, supported by technological developments.

PP. 442–447

COLLINS

wearecollins.com

COLLINS is a strategy and brand experience design company with offices in New York and San Francisco. It creates products, environments, and communications that transform brands, drive businesses, and improve lives.

PP. 066–069

Daniel Barkle

behance.net/Danbarkle

Daniel is a London-based graphic designer whose skills lie in typography, print, and music design. He is the co-founder of the Dank Type, a curated design platform that gives exposure to the highest forms of typography.

PP. 114–117, 326–333

Dasha F

far-studio.es

Dasha F is an artist from Moscow who loves the colour pink.

Davy Evans

davyevans.co.uk

Davy is an award-winning multi-disciplinary artist and designer based in Brighton. Armed with his background in graphic design, he fuses analogue and digital techniques to create ethereal, abstract imagery. He often uses experimental photographic methods combined with light and liquid in an attempt to replicate elements found in the natural world.

Dawn Creative

dawncreative.co.uk

Dawn Creative is a branding, design, digital, and motion agency. They wake up and shake up brands to make them fit and ready for the day ahead — like a shot of espresso. They are 'where stories are born and ideas shine brighter'.

DE_FORM Design Agency

de-form.hu

DE_FORM is a design agency and creative team founded by Nóra Demeczky and Enikő Déri specialising in branding, art direction and communication. They work on graphic systems for cultural events, institutions, designers, films, music labels, festivals, and more.

PP. 608–609

Design Ranch

design-ranch.com

Design Ranch has been creating and reinvigorating forward-thinking brands for years. They drive results with sincere, compelling, and creative messages that are designed to build brand presence, awareness, and mindshare.

PP. 228–231

dn&co.

dnco.com

dn&co. is a brand and design consultancy inspired by culture and place. They have worked with some of the world's leading architects, developers, planners, and cultural leaders to create meaningful destinations and neighbourhoods.

PP. 526–533

ECAL/University of Art and Design Lausanne

ecal.ch

ECAL or the École Cantonale d'Art de Lausanne is a university of art and design based in Renens, and is one of the top 10 in its field. ECAL's influence is reflected in numerous press articles and awards, exhibitions in prestigious venues, collaborations with well-known companies as well as the success of its graduates.

PP. 032–033, 130–133

Established

establishednyc.com

Established was set up in 2007 by Sam O'Donahue and Becky Jones. A full-service boutique agency, they offer graphic design, branding, art direction and packaging design services, with a track record of creating highly-successful, award-winning global brands for a wide range of clients.

PP. 296–299

Everyday Practice

everyday-practice.com

Everyday Practice was founded by Kwon Joonho, Kim Kyungchul, Kim Eojin and a small community thinking about the role of design in the real world. Although based in graphic design, the studio doesn't restrict its work to the two-dimensional space – experimenting with various design methods and applying its new-found knowledge to all of its work.

PP. 022–023, 510–511

Evin Tison

Evin is a young fashion designer who specialises in womenswear seeking to materialise the vision of a new couture in collaboration with art. Out of the usual codes, Evin's work is sculptural and provides audiences with a conceptual way to appreciate clothes.

Flov Creative Agency
flov.co

Flov Creative Agency is based in Wroclaw. They are a part of NOMONO, a strategic brand consultancy, design studio, and production company that fuses strong conceptual thinking with rigorous attention to detail to create timeless and effective work.

fontdesuka

fontdesuka is a project by graphic designer Mio Kuroiwa to experiment with typography. From 2018, she began a lettering project with the theme "the observation of letters". She produces client work such as brand logos, title logos and goods.

Foreign Policy Design Group

foreignpolicy.design

Foreign Policy in Singapore is an award-winning design bureau and think tank of artists, scientists, problem-solvers, polymaths, storytellers, and strategists translating today's ideas into tomorrow's experiences.

Formafantasma

formafantasma.com

Formafantasma is a research-based design studio investigating the ecological, historical, political and social forces shaping the discipline of design today. The studio applies the same rigorous attention to context, processes and details for each project. Formafantasma's analytical nature translates in meticulous visual outcomes, products and strategies.

François OLLIVIER

francoisollivier.com

François Ollivier is a photographer and visual artist who lives and works in Montreal. He has a knack for bringing meaning to the mundane through his candid or sometimes formally constructed compositions. He is a contributor for The New York Times, GQ, Vice, Monocle or Le Monde Magazine to name a few.

Fundamental

fundamental-studio.com

Fundamental is a Hong Kong-based creative studio with the belief that substantial communication is the key to creating and providing the best designs and solutions to clients.

PP. 288–291, 300–305

Futura

byfutura.com

Futura was founded in 2008 by Vicky González and Iván García. The intersection of two different backgrounds and working methods has given them a unique way of approaching projects, while finding balance between stiffness and rebellion.

PP. 098–103, 496–499

Glas Italia

glasitalia.com

Glas Italia was established in Brianza in the early 1970s. Driven by an unbridled passion for glass manufacturing, they produce modern pieces of furniture, door-wall partitions, and accessories in crystal glass — drawing from years of experience and technical know-how.

PP. 590–597

Greta Thorkels

behance.net/gretathorkels

Greta is an Icelandic graphic designer based in Berlin. She graduated with a BA degree in Visual Communication in 2016, with a background in Fine Arts. Currently, she focuses on art direction, editorial and music design.

PP. 438–441

HATTERN, UMZIKIM

hattern.com

Hattern is a product brand that exemplifies the beauty of ombre colours and material combinations. It was brought to life under the art direction of Jae Yang, who currently works between Seoul and Milan under UMZIKIM.

PP. 578–585

Hey

heystudio.es

Hey is a creative studio in Barcelona that creates fresh brands, conceptual communication campaigns, unique illustrations, and other creative outcomes by building strong relationships and taking care of every aspect of the design process. It believes in the power of visuals for changing things and achieving goals.

PP. 458–461, 484–491

Holiland

behance.net/a10047581976624GDD

Dong is a designer at Holiland specialising in brand and packaging design who likes to bring new and interesting things to everyone.

PP. 154–161

Hovercraft Studio

hovercraftstudio.com

Hovercraft Studio is an independent creative studio with offices in Portland and Denver. Their work is brand-centric and focuses on environments, retail and interactive experiences as well as site-specific installations.

PP. 274–277

HuskyFox

huskyfox.com

HuskyFox is a consultancy specialising in building brands through storytelling, art direction, identity design and visual systems. They address clear answers and sustain appropriate value and experiences. The BTS 'LOVE YOURSELF' project's main participants were Doohee Lee, Kiyoung Jung, and Hyuncheol Ahn

PP. 038–047

Irradié

irradie.com

L'atelier Irradié is a multi-disciplinary creative studio founded in 2016 by brothers Alain and Laurent Vonck. They offer visual and conceptual solutions in graphic design, art direction, and digital design. Their focus is on branding, graphical systems, publications, and digital interfaces for a variety of clients with intellectual curiosity and passion.

PP. 134–141, 470–475

K LASER Design Lab.

klasergroup.com

K LASER Design Lab. is a division established to promote holographic material applications through graphic design. Supported with the market's newest holographic effects, K LASER Design Lab. shares their creativity and applications to inspire global brands and design industry.

PP. 318–319

Kati Forner Design

katiforner.com

Kati is a Los Angeles-based creative director with years of experience in print and digital design. Rooted in classical design and forms, she creates a blend of minimal yet impactful work.

PP. 010–015

Kimgarden

kimgarden.kr

Kimgarden is a Seoul-based graphic design studio founded by Lee Yun Ho and Kim Kang In. They work with companies, museums, artists, and publishers in various fields. Fuelled by their strong interest in gardening, they have also designed gardening-related products.

PP. 312–317

Kolory

kolory.co

Kolory is a design and print studio based in Kraków. They aim to create designs that audiences would 'want to keep holding in their hands', or cannot take their eyes away from. Besides veering towards things that are light, clear, and well designed, they enjoy experimenting with print by combining seemingly incompatible materials, textures, and techniques.

PP. 016–021

Lundgren+Lindqvist

lundgrenlindqvist.se

Lundgren+Lindqvist is a Swedish design studio led by Andreas Friberg Lundgren and Carl-Johan Lindqvist. It has built an international reputation for crafting high-quality solutions that are equally compelling to the eyes and the intellect. The duo also runs Il'Editions, a publishing platform and imprint for creative cross-disciplinary collaborations.

PP. 320–325, 360–365

Machineast

machineast.com

Machineast is an independent creative design studio
that focuses on 3D typography and graphic design. They
have collaborated with many creative studios, advertising
agencies, and brands worldwide. Driven by a great passion
for making things aesthetically pleasing, Machineast always
does its best to offer creative solutions.

PP. 390–393

Marcin Wysocki

marcinwysocki.pl

Marcin is a designer who graduated from the Academy of
Fine Arts in Katowice. His portfolio includes visual identifi-
cation projects, books, posters, web applications, and video
clips. Besides working as an art director over the years,
he has been managing the publishing department of the
Centre for Contemporary Art (Kronika) since 2011.

PP. 232–233

Mariana Cecilia Iriberri

behance.net/marianairi

Mariana is a graphic designer who graduated from Univer-
sidad de Buenos Aires (UBA). She considers herself to be a
curious and observant person with a constant need to learn
and search for new experiences. Her passion lies in music
and visual expressions.

PP. 538–547

Marina Lewandowska

behance.net/lewmarina

Marina is currently working as a graphic designer in Vienna.
After graduating in 2017, she was an intern at Eduardo Aires
Studio in Portugal. She also worked at the Oskar Zięta-run
Zieta Prozessdesign studio while she was studying at the
Wroclaw Academy of Art and Design.

PP. 452–457

Mateusz Witczak

mateuszwitczak.com

Mateusz is a self-taught lettering artist and graphic designer
based in Warsaw. Besides specialising in detailed
hand-drawn lettering and typography designs that combine
traditional methods with the latest digital applications,
he is experienced in branding, packaging, textile design
and illustration.

PP. 292–295

Martin Tremblay

lepinch.com

Martin has an exceptional eye for the play between shadow
and light, making him a master at constructing hyper-re-
alistic images. He is an award-winning photographer
whose work has been recognised globally and published in
prestigious international magazines such as Zink New York,
Schön! London, NOI.SE Australia and Highlights Australia.

PP. 170–175

Michael Thorsby

michaelthorsby.com

Michael is a Paris-based graphic designer originally from
Sweden. Having travelled across a variety of cities, he has
picked up a myriad of creative influences to develop a style
that is unique to his background and experiences.

PP. 466–469

Michelle Tiquet Cardenas

Michelle is a Mexican graphic designer specialising in branding, editorial, and set design.

PP. 142–145

Midnight Design

mdnt.work

Midnight Design consists of a team of talented designers
from various fields. They devote themselves to brainstorming
and interweaving creative ideas all through the night for
extraordinary designs. To accomplish their mission through
unique perspectives and dynamic analysis, they dedicate
their time to solving client dilemmas.

PP. 142–145

Milkxhake

milkxhake.org

Milkxhake is an independent graphic design studio founded by Chinese graphic designer Javin Mo. Milkxhake advocates the power of visual communication from visual branding, identity, print, and website.

PP. 246–253

Mubien

mubien.com

Mubien is a design and handmade production studio-workshop based in Santander. Besides specialising in branding, corporate identity, and handmade productions, they enjoy researching new formulas, combinations and techniques to apply onto their work.

PP. 122–129

nendo

nendo.jp

Founded by architect Oki Sato in 2002, nendo in Tokyo sets out to bring small surprises to people through multidisciplinary practices of different media including architecture, interiors, furniture, industrial products, and graphic design.

PP. 574–577

Nonverbal Club

nonverbalclub.pt

Nonverbal Club is a design studio, based in Porto and Berlin. They focus on providing custom design solutions and communication consultancy to clients looking for work that goes beyond their expectations. Every project that they undertake is a dedicated balancing act between craft and technology, rationality and poetry, as well as expectation and surprise.

PP. 254–257

Not Available Design

behance.net/notavailable

Not Available Design is a multi-disciplinary studio focused on branding, design strategy, and space design. Founded by Kit Cheuk and Billy Sung, they serve innovative and creative clients who love to inject playful and unexpected twists on everyday simplicity. Their philosophy is NOT following a set routine AVAILABLE in the market, and daring to be different.

PP. 176–181

Noviki

noviki.net

Noviki lives in a graphic utopia. The studio's signature style is a context-driven approach based on the idea of design as a source for searching and exploring fields of contemporary artistic expression. Their works span across various media formats, from books and typefaces to exhibition design, videos, and applications.

PP. 366–369

Packvision

packvision.ru

Packvision is a Russian design studio that specialises in developing packaging and labels. They actively apply holographic materials onto their designs and think of them as the basis for new ideas.

PP. 054–057

PALAST PHOTOGRAPHIE — Julien Palast

julien.palast.fr

Julien is a French photographer based in Paris. His artistic work revolves around the body-object, reification, and fetishisation. His studio work revolves around still-lifes with retoucher Thierry Palast, for clients such as Baccarat, Clarins, Roger&Gallet, and Caudalie.

PP. 412–413

Paperlux Studio

paperlux.com

Paperlux Studio was established in 2006, and consists of an unconventional team of branding experts, purebred designers, material fetishists, and project wizards in Hamburg. Their creations constantly evolve in an environment that combines a studio, office, and workshop for German and international brands.

PP. 284–287

Parámetro Studio

parametro.studio

Parámetro Studio is a multi-disciplinary design practice based. They are all about becoming something new and iconic.

PP. 048–053

Paul Friedlander

paulfriedlander.com

Paul is a London-based scientific artist who first trained as a physicist with a degree from Sussex University, where his personal tutor, Tony Leggett subsequently received the Nobel prize for his works on superfluids. He continues to have a lively interest in the sciences which informs and shapes his work.

PP. 534–537

Pengguin

pengguin.hk

Pengguin is a multi-disciplinary design studio in Hong Kong that focuses on visual communication, branding, editorial projects, spatial and exhibition design as well as motion and interactive design. The studio's work has been recognised and published internationally.

PP. 104–107

Pentagram

pentagram.com

Pentagram is the world's largest independently owned design studio. Their work encompasses graphics, architecture, interiors, products, packaging, exhibitions, installations, digital experiences, advertising and communications.

Peter Tarka

petertarka.com

Peter is an art director and illustrator who creates CGI work that has viewers leaning in for a closer look. Having worked with clients such as Nike, BMW, Audi, Google, and more, the London-based creative has recently completed personal projects that showcase his talent for creating 3D illustrations.

PONYO PORCO

ponyoporco.com

PONYO PORCO is a brand that focuses on hand-painted printing. Launched in 2015, it was named after the founder's two axolotls, which are also featured on its logo to reflect the harmony and differences between individuals, as well as the brand philosophy.

Porto Rocha

portorocha.com

PORTO ROCHA is a New York-based design studio developing creative and strategic work that engages deeply with the world we live in. It seeks to provoke meaningful change through our work.

PP. 278–279

PRYSME

prysme.fr

PRYSME is a Bordeaux-based graphic design studio that values aesthetics, quality, and customisation. They base their creative ideas on their passion for beautiful papers, photography, and tailor-made websites.

PP. 334–337

Pyramid

studio-pyramid.com

Pyramid is a visual communication and sound design studio working for the music, arts, and culture sectors based in London and Lisbon. They are committed to using graphic design as a tool to always inquire about the world.

PP. 420–423

Radmir Volk

radmirvolk.design

Radmir specialises in brand design and is based in Moscow. He is a member of the AIGA and focuses on simple, clean, and timeless aesthetics.

Rus Khasanov

ruskhasanov.com

Rus Khasanov is a visual artist. His work is driven by the motto «Beauty is everywhere» which Rus expresses in music videos, typography and illustrations. The ability to express strong emotions through visual art, experimentation and improvisation plays a central role in his creative process.

Saerom Yoon

saeromyoon.com

Saerom is an artist who is inspired by the effortless beauty of nature, particularly the colours of the sunset and sunrise. To that end, he aspires for his sculptural furniture to have the appearance and feel similar to a watercolour painting.

selgascano

selgascano.net

selgascano is an intentionally-small atelier that has worked
on a wide variety of projects with nature at the core of the
programme. Established in 1998, they 'listen' to the largest
possible number of elements involved at every stage. They
strive to seek beauty that is universally comprehensible.

Selina Gerber

selinagerber.ch

Selina is an aspiring graphic designer who loves to experiment with colours, shapes, and typography. She also enjoys
expressing her talent for drawing with illustrations that
range from the witty to the ambitious.

Semiotik Design Agency

semiotikdesign.com

Semiotik Design Agency relies on simplicity, functionality,
and effectiveness strongly associated with emotional
responsiveness. Their design methodology is research-
based and aligned with the objectives of each project.

Shuka Design

shuka.design

Shuka Design is a cosy design studio based in Moscow that tailors visual identities and illustrations, produces websites and makes books. They are renowned for creating the controversial London World Chess Championship 2018 visual identity.

Siddhant Jaokar

hyperthalamuscorp.com

Siddhant is an industrial designer-turned-visual artist based in Mumbai. He believes in creating human experiences.

Sion Hsu Graphic

behance.net/sionhsu

Sion Hsu is a designer who is devoted to redesigning rural culture. Based in a small village called Tun Yuan Zih, he tries to show the world how beautiful his hometown is through his work. He believes that design should be accessible and everywhere.

Six N. Five

sixnfive.com

Six N. Five is a contemporary art duo based in Barcelona. Founded by Andy Reisinger and Ezequiel Pini, they specialise in still-life visuals with a clean, modern aesthetic. Aside from working on advertising and editorial commissions, they also find time to create experimental work that legitimises CGI as the new medium for creative self-expression.

Studio AH—HA

behance.net/studioahha

Founded by Carolina Cantante and Catarina Carreiras in 2011, Studio AH—HA is a graphic design and communication studio that focuses on brand strategy, visual identities, advertising, new media, photography, product design, and illustration. With different collaborators, they turn their clients' ideas into fresh and engaging messages.

Studio Band

studioband.com.au

Studio Band believes in brutally beautiful design. Their ethos is based on communicating and resonating with their clients and audiences. They offer creative yet effective solutions that are reached through intelligent understanding of the task at hand.